GLYNDEBOURNE
Festival Opera

1989

Founded in 1934 by Audrey and John Christie

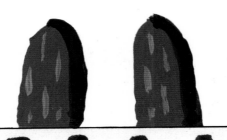

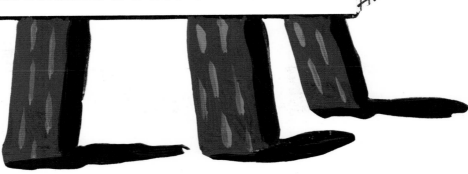

L Janáček
JENŮFA

C W Gluck
ORFEO ED EURIDICE

B Britten
A MIDSUMMER NIGHT'S DREAM

W A Mozart
LE NOZZE DI FIGARO

R Strauss
ARABELLA

I Stravinsky
THE RAKE'S PROGRESS

Guy Gravett

George Christie and Anthony Whitworth–Jones

FOREWORD

by George Christie
Chairman: Glyndebourne Productions Limited

There might seem, inadvertently, to be a cultural exchange afoot between Toronto and Glyndebourne. Brian Dickie goes to Toronto to take up the position of General Director of the Canadian Opera Company and Andrew Davis comes from the Toronto Symphony Orchestra as our new Musical Director.

Brian Dickie came to Glyndebourne in 1962 fresh from Trinity College, Dublin. His cousin, Hayman Dickie (a senior partner in Freshfields), contacted me at the time and asked whether there might be any room for his young musically devout relation to sharpen his teeth at Glyndebourne. I passed the message on to the correct quarter, the chief executive (Moran Caplat); and Mr Dickie was duly taken on as assistant to the Head of Music Staff, Jani Strasser, who shaped the start of his career to good effect. In 1967 we established the Glyndebourne Touring Opera and Brian Dickie was put in charge of this company. Later that year I was rung by the Chairman of the Wexford Festival, Sir Alfred Beit, and asked whether I knew of anyone who could suitably run that Festival, because the Artistic Director designate there, Walter Legge (of Philharmonia and EMI fame), had had a heart attack. I proposed Mr Dickie

who got the job and combined it with his administration of our spring tours for the next 7 years. From 1974 his chief concern was Glyndebourne, and in 1981 on Moran Caplat's retirement as General Administrator, Mr Dickie, the heir apparent, took on the principal role which he held until the end of 1988 with great distinction.

Glyndebourne now is still largely 'independent' and in remarkably good health artistically and economically and this in large measure is due to Mr Dickie's administrative skills. There can be a tendency for a person promoted from the position of 'second in command' to stick to the mould and context of the organisation in which he has been brought up. Mr Dickie instead approached the task with a refreshing and invigorating attitude, introduced changes at a wide variety of levels and brought Glyndebourne abreast of the 1980s. More than anything, his administrative regime will, in my view, be remembered for the artistic standards he has aimed for – and achieved. His influence on the choice of repertory, conductors, directors and singers has been pervasive and the achievement of Glyndebourne's present artistic reputation must to a major extent be attributed to him.

The choice of Mr Dickie's successor has been made amidst stiff competition and has fallen on Anthony Whitworth-Jones who has effectively been Mr Dickie's 'number two' in the last 8 years. An extensive search was launched for a suitable successor and the choice has come full circle – a fact which must reinforce the aptness of the appointment. He has my – and to his credit, I believe, the Company's – heartfelt wishes now as 'number one'.

Bernard Haitink was courted by the Royal Opera House and took up the musical reins there last autumn. Andrew Davis, whose operatic pedigree is largely Glyndebourne-based (*Capriccio, Eugene Onegin, Schweigsame Frau, Zauberflöte, Falstaff, Arabella, Don Giovanni* and *Kát'a Kabanová*) and whose symphonic pedigree is largely North-American-

2

based came on to the market on his departure as Musical Director of the Toronto Symphony and we were quick to snap him up in succession to Mr Haitink. It was like finding that tangerine at the toe of the Christmas stocking: you know there is a good chance that it is going to be there and, when you find it, it leaves a good taste in the mouth. Long may that last.

This Festival sees the introduction of the Orchestra of the Age of Enlightenment, an orchestra which over the next few years will perform the cycle of new productions of Mozart/da Ponte operas at Glyndebourne under Simon Rattle. There is an increasing curiosity amongst audiences to hear music of the eighteenth and earlier centuries on its terms rather than necessarily on our twentieth century terms. This is not intended in the case of Glyndebourne's employment of the OAE to consign such music to the 'museum'. In fact precisely the reverse is intended – namely to provide an alternative sound where, for example, the expression of the music's passion can be given vent to at least as effectively with period instruments as can be achieved with the more full-bodied and consequently more overwhelming effect of modern instruments. The fact that you have in a sense to work more vigorously with period instruments to convey the drama of the music means that the players can in some degree let rip without fear of upsetting the balance of sound between stage and pit. All of this may go against the grain as far as concerns those wedded to the sound developed on modern instruments, but, with the current re-emergence of period instruments and with Simon Rattle's enthusiasm for this renaissance, it would be churlish or perverse of Glyndebourne to appear to be entrenched in its advocacy of performances with modern instruments only – and would be totally bereft of any visionary (or do I mean audio?) aspirations.

Bankers Trust – I am, on our collective behalf, enormously grateful to say – agreed to give valuable sponsorship to assist Glyndebourne to engage the OAE in 1989.

The London Philharmonic will of course continue as the principal orchestra in this and future Festivals, undertaking the vast majority of the repertory here.

Glyndebourne is much indebted to its sponsors, in particular to the sponsors of the new productions – Allied-Lyons in the case of *Jenůfa* and Waterford Wedgwood in the case of *Figaro* this year. Without such sponsorship Glyndebourne's repertory would dry up and the future would indeed look barren. Without Sir Alex Alexander, Deputy Chairman of Allied Lyons, sponsorship not just of *Jenůfa* but of the majority of Glyndebourne's new productions in the past twelve years could be called into question. Glyndebourne also has grounds for considerable gratitude for English & American Group's sponsorship of the revival of *The Rake's Progress*.

It is with sadness, but gratitude that I record here the retirement of Lord Richardson and Mr R A Garrett as Trustees. The irony is they belie their years and their evergreen contribution to Glyndebourne bears witness to this. (Lord Richardson, however, remains on the Finance Committee.) At the same time I am specially pleased to announce the appointments of Sir Claus Moser and Sir David Scholey to the Trust. Their diverse and distinguished careers and interests can hardly help but enhance hugely the diversity and distinction of the make-up of the Trust.

Finally, on the question of enlarging the theatre here, I can report – at the time of writing this – that we are on the verge of choosing an architect and that, subject to the agreement of the Boards of Directors and Trustees to pursue the idea, we will during the course of 1989 assess the financial feasibility of converting it into a reality. I can only say at this stage that the 'design concepts' presented by the two short-listed architects provide in each case the answers to a large number of difficulties relating to Glyndebourne's operation over the next fifty years – and I would not wish the problem of having to make a choice between these two excellent architects on any friend.

Hurricane Help

Contributions to the 'tree pot' following the 1987 storm have been generously given by:

Dr W G Baker	Mr Bernard Levin
Mr James Bettley	Mr James Lister
Mr R L Calder	The London Philharmonic
Richard Ellis	Miss Janet Moores MBE
Mr Stewart Finch	Miss Johanna Peters
The Guildhall School of Music	Mr E K Roberts
and Drama	Mr Douglas Webster
Lt Col and Mrs P K Hill	Mr and Mrs A E Yuill
Mr John S Hilton	Trustees of the Glyndebourne
In memory of Harry Kellard	Arts Trust
	and others

The effects of the long haul to recovery are just beginning to emerge.
George Christie

A TRIBUTE TO
SIR ALEX ALEXANDER

on his retirement as a Trustee

Since writing the Foreword, I have learned with the greatest chagrin of Sir Alex Alexander's retirement from the Glyndebourne Arts Trust. My vocabulary does not possess the words to express with anything approaching adequacy Glyndebourne's irredeemable debt to him. He has, like nobody else in Glyndebourne's history, changed our fortunes. He has not only introduced considerable sponsorship here; he has radically and constructively adjusted Glyndebourne's financial frame of mind.

He joined the Trust in 1974 and soon after became Vice-Chairman. He has also been Chairman of the Finance Committee and a Director of Glyndebourne Productions Limited. His influence has been pervasive like no other non-executive's. He has commanded the respect and gratitude of all of us working at Glyndebourne and, I am sure, of all of you whose interests he has so valuably served. The cost of performances would be less attainable for you and less containable for us, but for Sir Alex.

The Trust loses a remarkable man and a friend who is irreplaceable.

GC

A chronological record of major sponsorship of new productions and revivals

(the years referred to are those for which the sponsorship was granted).

Past sponsorship of productions and revivals

The Peter Stuyvesant Foundation: 7 new productions and 5 revivals between 1966 and 1981.

The Fred Kobler Trust: *Intermezzo* 1974, *La fedeltà premiata* 1979.

The Fred Kobler Trust/The Corbett Foundation of Cincinatti: *Falstaff* 1976.

The Henry & Lily Davis Charitable Trust: *Pelléas et Mélisande* 1976.

Imperial Tobacco Limited/John Player & Sons: *Don Giovanni* 1977, *Die Zauberflöte* 1978, *Fidelio* 1979, *Der Rosenkavalier* 1980, *Il barbiere di Siviglia* 1981, *Orfeo ed Euridice* 1982, *Arabella* 1984.

National Westminster Bank: *Così fan tutte* 1978, *La Cenerentola* 1983.

Dresdner Bank AG/Deutsche BP AG: *Die Entführung aus dem Serail* 1980.

Commercial Union Assurance Company Limited: *A Midsummer Night's Dream* 1981.

Cointreau SA: *L'Amour des Trois Oranges* 1982.

Autobar Group Limited: *Idomeneo* 1983.

IBM United Kingdom Limited: *L'incoronazione di Poppea* 1984, *L'heure espagnole/L'enfant et les sortilèges* 1987.

Pearson: *Where the Wild Things Are* 1984, *Higglety Pigglety Pop!* 1985.

Autobar Group Limited/Hays Group Limited: *Albert Herring* 1985.

Citicorp Investment Bank Ltd: *Carmen* 1985, *Porgy and Bess* 1986.

Honeywell Limited: *Simon Boccanegra* 1986.

B.A.T Industries: *La traviata* 1987.

ICI: *Capriccio* 1987 (revival).

Vincent Meyer: *The Electrification of the Soviet Union* (for GTO) 1987.

Castrol: *Falstaff* 1988.

The Philip & Pauline Harris Charitable Trust: *Kát'a Kabanová* 1988.

Present and future sponsorship of productions

Allied-Lyons: *Jenůfa* 1989.

Waterford Wedgwood: *Le nozze di Figaro* 1989.

English & American Group plc: *The Rake's Progress* 1989 (revival).

Hays Group Limited: *Death in Venice* (for GTO) 1989.

Deutsche Bank: *The Magic Flute* 1990.

Imry Merchant Developers: Michael Tippett's *New Year* 1990.

IBM United Kingdom Trust: *La clemenza di Tito* 1991.

Castrol: *Così fan tutte* 1991.

Other major sponsorship of productions

W D & H O Wills: for maintenance of buildings and gardens 1976–1980.

Barclays Bank plc: Glyndebourne Touring Opera 1983–1988.

The Miller Family: EMI recording of *Don Giovanni* 1984.

Vincent Meyer: EMI recordings of *Così fan tutte* 1987, *Le nozze di Figaro* 1988.

Banker's Trust: Orchestra of the Age of Enlightenment for performances of *Figaro* 1989.

The Glyndebourne Chorus Scheme

The Glyndebourne Chorus helps to bridge the gap which exists between a young singer's departure from a College of Music and subsequent arrival as a recognised soloist. It fulfils this function by providing young singers with the opportunity of working in the Festival and Touring companies as choristers and understudies and in certain cases as soloists in the Glyndebourne Touring Opera from which they may achieve soloist status in the Festival. It is not a permanent body as such but is recruited annually and is made up of young aspiring soloists. As well as participating in the Glyndebourne Festival and the Glyndebourne Touring Opera, the Chorus from time to time takes part in concerts, gramophone recordings and both sound and television broadcasts. The training that singers derive from the work they undertake as choristers and understudies at Glyndebourne is therefore of considerable importance to the operatic profession of which Britain remains internationally in the forefront.

The financial support of this scheme has considerably helped to mitigate the burden of the Festival's rising costs. This is the thirteenth year in which this Scheme has operated. During this period the funds raised have gratifyingly multiplied four-fold. Glyndebourne is much indebted to all who are generously supporting the Scheme.

The following are full supporters of the Glyndebourne Chorus Scheme:

Allied Lyons PLC
The Baring Foundation
Bass PLC
The Bird Charitable Trust
Bunzl PLC
Chloride Group PLC
Sir Edmund G Compton GCB, GBE
D'Arcy Masius Benton & Bowles
Davidson Pearce Limited
C H W Dixon Charitable Trust
Drexel Burnham Lambert
Esso UK plc
Gartmore Investment Management Limited
The Godinton Charitable Trust
Guinness PLC
Imperial Chemical Industries PLC
The Jane Hodge Foundation
R J Kiln & Co Limited
The Linbury Trust
The Manor Charitable Trust
Marks and Spencer PLC
Marley PLC
The Mercers' Company
The Nestlé Charitable Trust
Ogilvy & Mather Limited
Philips Electronics
Mr Nigel Porter
Ranks Hovis McDougall PLC
Reckitt & Colman PLC
The Rio Tinto-Zinc Corporation PLC
Mr & Mrs D Secker Walker
Shell UK Limited
Swire Charitable Trust
Unigate PLC

The following have also made generous contributions towards the Chorus Scheme:

Mrs V L Knox
Morgan Guaranty Trust Co
Jocelyne and Julian Tobin

Musical Preparation

To coin a platitude, the quality of musical preparation determines to a large degree the quality of an opera house's performance. Glyndebourne is an ensemble theatre in the sense that it is not geared to provide a vehicle for star singers. The works of Mozart have traditionally formed the backbone of the repertory here and will continue to do so. These works like the rest of Glyndebourne's repertory require meticulous attention to detail during the course of long periods of rehearsals – a characteristic which has always been exemplified by Glyndebourne. It is on this aspect of its work that Glyndebourne stakes a very large measure of its reputation.

The team responsible for musical preparation is largely made up of established and young aspiring conductors and musicians engaged on a seasonal basis. The cost of their engagement for the six productions customarily staged in each Festival will amount in 1989 to £148,500. It is towards this cost that support is sought and towards the continued maintenance of musical standards that such support is needed.

This scheme also provides frequently for an award for a young conductor or repetiteur drawn from the Glyndebourne team. The award is named after the late Head of Music Staff, Jani Strasser and is given to help further the career of a specially talented young musician requiring a period of study. The award was given last autumn to the repetiteur David Gowland. Previous recipients have been Christopher Willis, Jonathan Burton, Jane Robinson and Ivor Bolton.

The start of this scheme in 1981 was financed by Mr Helmut Rothenberg. He has continued to help the scheme generously and his example has been followed by a number of individuals and organisations.

The support in 1989 has been given by:

Mr Helmut Rothenberg
In memory of Robert J Ormond
Mr Thomas and Mr Gordon Black
Winchester Bowring Limited
Peter Stuyvesant Foundation
Tower Bridge Underwriting Agencies Ltd
Richard Lehr Charity
Helma Charitable Trust
Mr David Rothenberg
Mr Robert Rothenberg

Awards

The John Christie Award

The Worshipful Company of Musicians has, since 1965, made it possible, in collaboration with Glyndebourne, to award an annual scholarship to enable a young and promising singer from the Glyndebourne company to study abroad. The 1988 Award was made to Robert Poulton.

Previous holders have been:
Ryland Davies, Richard Van Allan, Jill Gomez, Teresa Cahill, Yvonne Fuller, Anthony Roden, Ian Caley, Linda Esther Gray, Elizabeth Gale, Anthony Rolfe Johnson, John Rawnsley, Kate Flowers, Fiona Kimm, Keith Lewis, Christopher Blades, Helen Walker, Glenn Winslade, John Hall, Louise Winter, Anna Steiger, Peter Rose, Alastair Miles.

The Esso Glyndebourne Touring Opera Singers' Award

This award was established in 1977 through the generosity of an anonymous private donor. In 1980 Esso made possible a further award for a young singer engaged by Glyndebourne. In 1983, when the private donor's covenant expired, Esso Exploration and Production UK Limited increased the amount of their support and assumed responsibility for the financing of the amalgamation of the two awards. The 1988 Award was made to Christopher Ventris.

Previous holders of these Awards have been Helen Walker, Mary King, Yvonne Lea, Hugh Hetherington, Catherine Benson, John Hall, Deborah Rees, Glenn Winslade, Anne Dawson, Louise Winter, Peter Coleman-Wright, Patrick Donnelly, Alastair Miles, Robert Poulton.

Glyndebourne Arts Trust

Glyndebourne wishes to record its sincere gratitude to the Trustees of the Arts Trust and to all those who have made convenants or donations to the Glyndebourne Festival in the past year.

The undermentioned have given support to an especially generous degree:

Support from the following has also been most gratefully received

Arthur Abeles Esq
Mrs R F Adams
W J Alsford Esq
Dr Y Anthony
Felix Appelbe Esq
P Armitage Esq
A S Ashby Esq
Mrs D M Ashurst
W T F Austin Esq
A Babington Smith Esq
Dr & Mrs William G Baker
Peter Baring Esq
Raymond Barnett Esq
B A Bates Esq
E G Beaumont Esq
Dr & Mrs E W Bedford Turner
The Michael Bernstein
    Charitable Trust
F H A Bex Esq
Mrs Sonia Bird
John A Bishopp Esq
L B Black Esq
L J Boon Esq
Mrs Simon Boosey
F H Boots Esq
Anthony Boswood Esq
J M Bowers Esq
Mrs Edith S Bowring
Peter Boydell Esq QC
K A Boyes Esq
John S Braithwaite Esq
S B Brayshaw Esq
The Hon Mrs Bridge
A F Briggs Esq
William L Brightwell Esq
A E Brooks Esq
Mrs M G J Brown
M Bryanston Esq
P J Bryant Esq
P J Bull Esq
N S D Bulmer Esq
Mr & Mrs S Eden Bushell
Mrs Jo Butler
P Butler Esq
A L Cable Esq
Ronald Calder Esq
Mrs C M Campbell
The Viscountess Camrose
S G Cantacuzino Esq
The Rt Hon The Lord Carr of
    Hadley
The Hon Anthony Cayzer
Mrs M F Cecil
David A Charlesworth Esq
Miss J M Bessemer Clark
Sir Robert Clark
R J Clark Esq
W K Clarke Esq
J W Clement Esq
The Gerald Coke Charitable
    Trust
G A Collens Esq
Norman H Collins Esq
Mrs C Cook
M E Cope Esq
A Coren Esq
Dr J Cotter
Mr & Mrs G M Cumberlege
Mrs Laura Davies

G G J Davis Esq
Miss D B Dearn
Mrs R J Dell
D P Derrington Esq
Mrs D M B Dibben
T H Drabble Esq
M C Dunlop Esq
Lady Dunnett
J C Edwards Esq
M J Edwards Esq
L Esterman Esq
J R Fenner Esq
D R Fendick Esq
J J Fenton Esq
Mrs M E S Ferrier
Carl E Fischer Esq
Mrs B Fisher
Prof Michael Földi
A H Foord Esq
Mr Richard E Ford
Col John M Forster
L A Foster Esq
A B Fothergill Esq
E Maxwell Fry Esq CBE
Gee Lawson Chemicals Ltd
W H Gervis Esq
The Lord Gibson
G E Gilchrist Esq
The Godinton Charitable Trust
D A Goldberg Esq
I A Goldstein Esq
G F Gomme Esq
Everard and Mina Goodman
    Charitable Foundation
Brandon Gough Esq
Mr & Mrs A P Graham-Dixon
S L Greaves Esq
A Wyndham Green Esq
Dr G W Green
J A Greenacre Esq
D S Greenfield Esq
J Greenfield Esq
W A L Griffith Esq
M W Hall Esq
Mr & Mrs R J P Hallam
T G C Halliwell Esq
Mrs B N Halpern
C G Headlam Esq
Mrs J A Hedley-Dent
The Lord Henniker
Peter Herbert Esq
Derek Hill Esq
D L Hodges Esq
Mrs J B Hodson
Sir John Hogg
J L Homfray Esq
G Horsfall Esq
Peter & Jane How
Neil Hughes-Onslow Esq
C P M Hunting Esq CBE
Lord Hutchinson QC
P C Hyde-Thomson Esq
M P Ingham Esq
R A Ingham Esq
D A Innes Esq
The Rt Hon Sir Bryant & Lady
    Godman Irvine
Mrs D H Irwin
G C Ives Esq

Mr & Mrs Victor R Jackson
Betty Lady Jessel
B Johnson Esq
Nicholas Johnston Esq
Mr & Mrs J I Karet
A Kemball Price Esq
The Lord Kissin of Camden
Mr & Mrs I S Klug
Mrs V L Knox
In memory of Mrs Sigrid Kuritz
Peter Leaver Esq QC
E A M Lee Esq
Mrs Doreen M Lester
P R S Lever Esq
Mr & Mrs M P Levesley
Mrs Richard Lewis
Miss Clare Lilleyman
S B S Livesey Esq
Raymond Lister Esq
L & C Lowenthal Charitable
    Trust
Mrs J Lyell
Dr Eileen Mackenzie
Mr & Mrs B McHenry
A J McKerracher Esq
Mrs James McNeish
G Mainzer Esq
Sir Charles Mander
F E Manning Esq
Sir Peter Marshall
Miss Ursula Maunsell
L Mechulam Esq
A L Merry Esq
Mrs F V Michell
P E Middleton Esq
R G Middleton Esq
Stanley Middleton Esq
D C St Clair Miller Esq
Montagu Ventures Ltd
S J Mosley Esq
Peter Murray Esq
Dr & Mrs S M Nemet
Mr R Newiss
J M Norsworthy Esq
W E Norton Esq
The Rt Hon The Lord O'Brien
    of Lothbury GBE, PC
J C F O'Moore Esq
Mrs M K D O'Moore
Lt Col Beville Pain
J A Paine Esq
E H Palmer Esq CBE
Mrs R G Parratt
T C Pasola Esq
G D B Pearse Esq
Dr & Mrs Jeremy Pfeffer
R Pfizenmaier Esq
R M Philips Esq
Mrs J M Piggott
A Pilcher Esq
Sir Dennis Pilcher CBE
G W Pingstone Esq
O A Proctor Esq
Dr M J Prophet
S D Rae Esq
J Rawson Holdings Ltd
R A & V B Reekie Charitable
    Trust
J R Reynolds Esq

Mr & Mrs Hugh Robinson
Miss Nina Robinson
D G Robson Esq
The Rogot Trust
Algernon Rothman Esq FCA
Jeremy Rothman
Rebecca Rothman
Simon Rothman
M G Royle Esq
The Hon Sir Steven Runciman
J R Salter Esq
T W Sandeman Esq
The E E Sander Charitable Trust
N P D Sarkari Esq
R Schlagman Esq
D L Scholte Esq
D W M Scott Esq
Sir Hilary Scott
Mrs J Lindsay Scott
S L Scott Esq
G W Searle Esq CBE DSC
D J B Seaton Esq
L R L Shadbolt Esq
Sir William Shapland
Dr A G Sharpe
Mrs F Shaw
Tom Shearer Esq CB
In memory of Lewis Simmons
R A S Sisterson Esq
F Solari Esq
P F Spencer Moore Esq
Mr L Stolzer-Cheyne
Mr & Mrs P S Strudwick
Mr & Mrs Reyneke van Stuwe
Mrs E D Sugden
Mr Robert E Sullivan
Mr & Mrs William M Sullivan
F G Sutherland Esq
Mrs J Talbot-Ponsonby
Mrs A Lacy Tate
Dr D L Taylor
Mr & Mrs J A G Taylor
D L Thornley Esq
H C Torbock Esq
U E I plc
W F W Urich Esq
L F B Vale Esq
D N Vermont Esq
J L Vernon Esq
R P Vickers Esq
R L Vigars Esq
Berkeley Walker-Carpenter
Nevile G Wallace Esq
Ronald Watts Esq
George Weston Esq
H Whitbread Esq
G I White Esq
Dr & Mrs J White
Mrs H Searle Whitmore
M E Willis-Fleming Esq
L J Windridge Esq
George C Winter Esq
J H G Woollcombe Esq
Dr Richard Wray
Mrs & Mrs G R Young
J R Young Esq
Dr R Youngman
Dr A Ywan

Glyndebourne Festival Society

Corporate Members

APV PLC
ASL/Alliance (London) Ltd
ASSI Pulp & Paper Sales (UK) Ltd
Abbey National Building Society
Advertising and Design Associates
Allen & Overy
Allen, Brady & Marsh Ltd
Allied Lyons PLC
Allied Leather Industries PLC
Amdahl (UK) Limited
Arthur Andersen & Co
Associated Newspapers Holdings PLC
Autobar Industries Limited
B.A.T Industries PLC
BFCS Ltd.
BICC PLC
BMP Davidson Pearce Limited
BPCC–MCC
The BOC Group PLC
The BP Group of Companies
Bain Clarkson Limited
Bank Julius Baer & Co Ltd
Barclays Bank PLC
Barings PLC
Bass PLC
Bechtel Ltd
Beecham Products
Billiton (UK) Limited
Borax Holdings Limited
C T Bowring & Co Ltd
British Gas PLC
British Steel PLC
British Sugar PLC
Britoil PLC
Brooke Bond Oxo Ltd
John Brown PLC
Bunzl PLC
Leo Burnett Limited
The Burton Group PLC
C L. Alexanders Laing & Cruickshank
    Holdings Ltd
Cable and Wireless PLC
Castrol (UK) Limited
Cazenove & Co
Charnos PLC
The Chase Manhattan Bank NA
Chloride Group PLC
Cimex Limited
Citicorp/Citibank
Clive Discount Company Limited
C J Coleman Holdings Limited
Collett, Dickenson, Pearce and
    Partners Ltd
Commercial Union Assurance
    Company PLC
Consolidated Gold Fields PLC
Continental Can Company (UK) Ltd
Costain Group PLC

Cow & Gate Limited
Credit Suisse First Boston Ltd
Cussins Green Properties PLC
D'Arcy Masius Benton & Bowles
Deloitte Haskins & Sells
Deutsche Bank AG
Donner Underwriting Agencies
    Limited
Drexel Burnham Lambert
    International Inc
English & American Group PLC
Esso UK PLC
EBC Amro Bank Limited
Eurobase Financial Services
Ewbank Preece Group Limited
Esmée Fairbairn Charitable Trust
Fenchurch Insurance Holdings Limited
Ferranti International Signal PLC
The First National Bank of Chicago
Foote, Cone & Belding Ltd
Ford of Europe Incorporated
Foster Wheeler Energy Limited
Freshfields
Gallaher Tobacco (UK) Limited
Gartmore Investment Management
    Limited
Glynwed International PLC
Goldman Sachs International Corp
Gouldens
Gresham Trust PLC
Guinness PLC
Guinness Mahon Holdings PLC
Sir Philip Harris
John Harvey & Sons Ltd
Hays PLC
C E Heath PLC
Hermes (GB) Ltd
High Duty Alloys (Properties) Ltd
Hightons
Hill Samuel Group PLC
Hoare Govett Ltd
Hogg Robinson & Gardner Mountain
    PLC
Honeywell Limited/Bull HN Information
    Systems Ltd
D R Hunnisett Esq
IBM United Kingdom Limited
Imperial Chemicals Industries PLC
Imperial Tobacco Limited
Imry Merchant Developers
ITM Corporation Limited
JS Associates
John Jenkins & Sons Limited
Michael and Ilse Katz Charitable Trust
The Kaye Organisation Limited
P W Kininmonth Limited
Kleinwort, Benson Limited
Kyle Stewart Limited

Laporte Industries (Holdings) PLC
Lazard Brothers & Co. Limited
Legal & General Group PLC
Letheby & Christopher Limited
John Lewis PLC
Lex Service PLC
Lintas: International
Llewellyn Homes Ltd
O W Loeb & Company Limited
L'Oreal
Y J Lovell (Holdings) PLC
Lucas Industries PLC
L'Union des Assurances de Paris
J Lyons & Company Limited
MGM Assurance
McCann-Erickson Advertising Ltd
R.A.F. Macmillan & Co Limited
Manufacturers Hanover Limited
Marks and Spencer PLC
Marley PLC
F W Mason & Sons Ltd
Matheson & Co Limited
The Medical Tribune Group
MB Group PLC
Midland Bank PLC
Thos R Miller & Son (Insurance)
J H Minet & Co Ltd
Mobil Services Company Limited
Monarch Investment Group
Samuel Montagu & Co Limited
The Peter Moores Foundation
Morgan Grenfell & Co Limited
Morgan Guaranty Trust Company
    of New York
Morgan Stanley International
Multicom Holdings Limited
National Westminster Bank PLC
The Nestlé Co. Ltd
Norton Rose
Occidental Financial Services Inc
Ogilvy & Mather Limited
R H M Outhwaite (Underwriting
    Agencies) Ltd
Pandrol International Ltd
Panmure Gordon and Co
Pearson PLC
Peat Marwick McLintock
Philipp & Lion Ltd
Philip Brothers Limited
Philips Electronics
J R Phillips & Co Ltd
Powell Duffryn PLC
Price Waterhouse
R P (Consultants) Ltd
The Rank Organisation PLC
Ranks Hovis McDougal PLC
Reckitt & Colman PLC
Reed Corrugated Cases

Index of Advertisers

A perfect partnership:
Waterford and Wedgwood

ENGLISH & AMERICAN GROUP
LONDON · NEW YORK · GLYNDEBOURNE

PRUDENTIAL

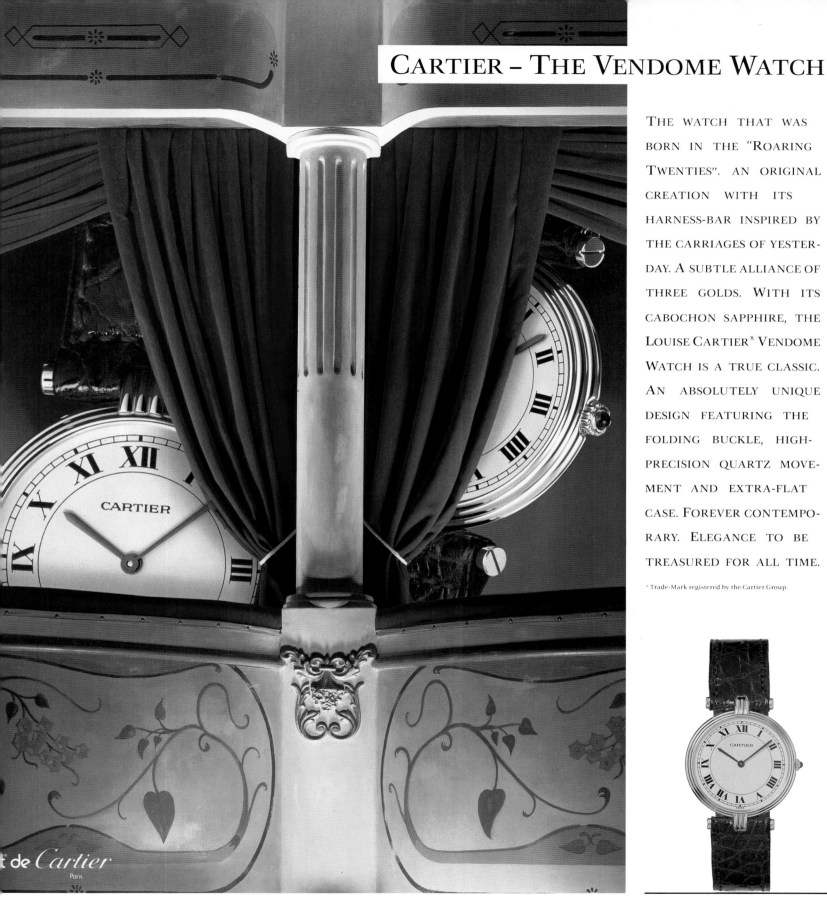

CARTIER – THE VENDOME WATCH

THE WATCH THAT WAS BORN IN THE "ROARING TWENTIES". AN ORIGINAL CREATION WITH ITS HARNESS-BAR INSPIRED BY THE CARRIAGES OF YESTERDAY. A SUBTLE ALLIANCE OF THREE GOLDS. WITH ITS CABOCHON SAPPHIRE, THE LOUISE CARTIER® VENDOME WATCH IS A TRUE CLASSIC. AN ABSOLUTELY UNIQUE DESIGN FEATURING THE FOLDING BUCKLE, HIGH-PRECISION QUARTZ MOVEMENT AND EXTRA-FLAT CASE. FOREVER CONTEMPORARY. ELEGANCE TO BE TREASURED FOR ALL TIME.

* Trade-Mark registered by the Cartier Group.

Cartier

L'ART D'ÊTRE UNIQUE

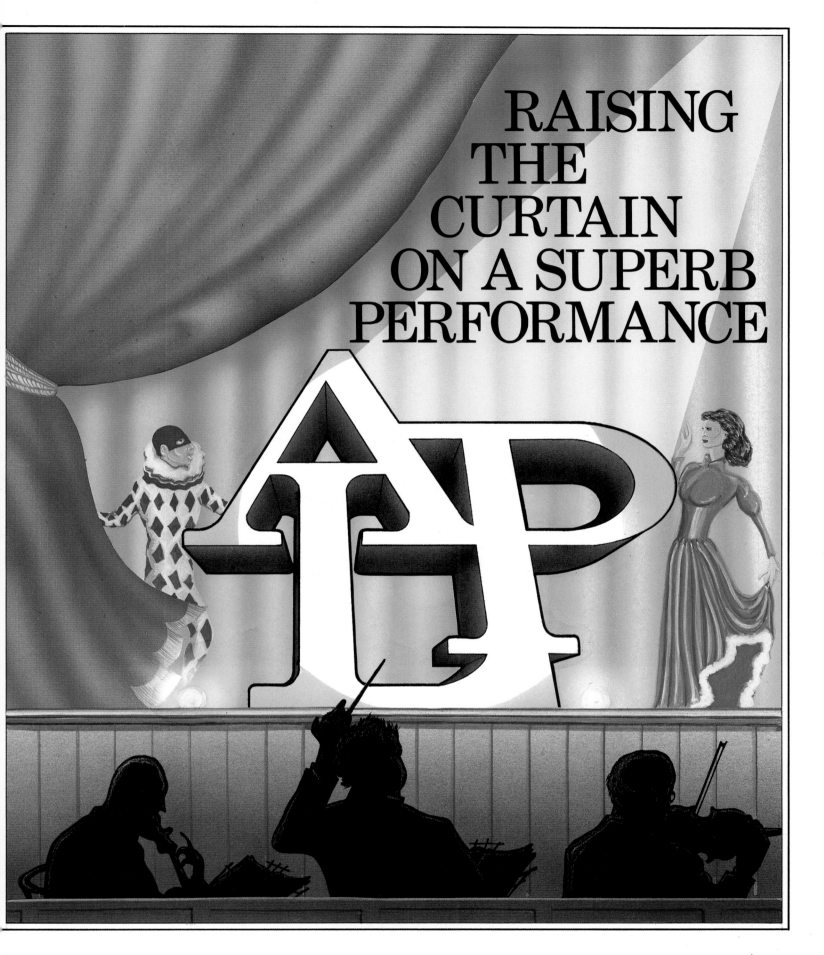

RAISING
THE
CURTAIN
ON A SUPERB
PERFORMANCE

Allied London Properties Plc

Allied House 26 Manchester Square London W1A 2HU

FOR SOME, LIFE'S TRUE VALUES ARE EASY TO RECOGNISE.

The Gold Card®

MOLTO VIVACE

SIERRA

Sierra orchestrated by Cosworth

CHANGE UP TO **PIONEER**®

IN-CAR STEREO

WHEN THE GUESSING HAS TO STOP

Sir Thomas Beecham.
Recognised for his services to music.

Hays plc.
Recognised for their services to business.

THE BUSINESS SERVICES GROUP

A Midsummer Night's Dream
at Glyndebourne

TATE GALLERY – TITANIA & BOTTOM BY HENRY FUSELI

Richard Ellis are helping the Glyndebourne dream come true

Richard Ellis

INTERNATIONAL PROPERTY CONSULTANTS

The Mercedes-Benz 190E 2.5-16: 197 bhp, 0 to 62 mph 7.5 seconds, top speed 143 mph (manufacturer's figures).

Der Rosenkavalier

ENGINEERED LIKE NO OTHER CAR IN THE WORLD.

The search for excellence stops here.

VANL
A worldwide commitment to oil.

Now it's time to play <u>your</u> part.

PLEASE SEND A DONATION, LARGE OR SMALL, TO:

MUSICIANS BENEVOLENT FUND

SIR IAN HUNTER, CHAIRMAN,

16 OGLE STREET, LONDON W1P 7LG.

This advertisement was donated by a Festival Society member in memory of her husband.

Till at last she set herself to man
Like Perfect Music unto Noble Words
And Rarest Treasure formed by Dextrous Hands.

(*After Alfred Lord Tennyson*)

M. Ekstein Ltd – I.J. Mazure & Co. Ltd.
90 Jermyn Street, Piccadilly, London SW1.
Tel. 01 930 2024 – 01 839 3101/2

THE SCALE OF OUR OPERATIONS

"Con Brio" by Kevin Holt.
One of a series of works by young artists commissioned by

CHATEAU LATOUR

Premier Grand Cru Classé ~ Pauillac

COCO

PARFUM ET EAU DE PARFUM DE CHANEL

Happily, this year, the community is over £10,000,000 better off.

This year, as in previous years, NatWest are taking an active role in the community. Over £10,000,000 has already been committed to a wide range of environmental, social, arts and sporting projects all over the country.

We don't just help with money either. More than 150 of our senior staff will be seconded to help with the day to day running of community projects, bringing with them all their experience and expertise in finance.

The community is something that includes everyone, so if our contribution can help improve it in any way, we at NatWest believe it's money well spent.

NatWest The Action Bank

P R E S S   F O R   A C T I O N

Dabinett

A Fine English Tradition.

FOR MORE THAN A HUNDRED YEARS H.P. BULMER HAVE BEEN CIDER MAKERS.
WE WOULD LIKE TO TAKE THIS OPPORTUNITY TO SALUTE ANOTHER DISTINGUISHED
CONTRIBUTOR TO THE ENGLISH SUMMER SCENE.

The Bellwinch plc Homes Group

Malcolm House, Empire Way, Wembley, Middlesex.

FOR PERFECTLY TUNED FORKS.

BY APPOINTMENT TO
HM THE QUEEN
MANUFACTURERS OF INDUSTRIAL TRUCKS
LANSING BAGNALL LTD BASINGSTOKE

LANSING LIMITED
KINGSCLERE ROAD, BASINGSTOKE
HAMPSHIRE RG21 2XJ
TELEPHONE: BASINGSTOKE (0256) 473131
TELEX: 858120 LBBA G

THE SEASON

A few essentials:

Champagne of the season.

Flora Danica. Created 200 years ago at the request of the Danish Royal Family, and still one of the greatest achievements of Danish craftsmanship. Flora Danica from Royal Copenhagen Porcelain. Acorn cutlery from Georg Jensen. Design: Johan Rohde. Eclair glasses from Holmegaard. Design: Ann Sofi Romme. Tokyo. Hong Kong. Singapore. New York. Paris. London. Copenhagen. Sydney.

Louis Vuitton. The art of travel.

L V The Louis Vuitton craftsmen possess the secret of constantly renewing tradition while maintaining all of its qualities. They fashion trunks, hard-sided and soft-sided luggage, accessories and small leather goods that quickly become new companions for news journeys. The famous initials are the stamp of authenticity of these unique skills.

Louis Vuitton. Exclusive stores:

London Mayfair, 149 New Bond Street, Tel. (01) 409 0155
London Knightsbridge, 198 Sloane Street, Tel. (01) 235 3356

LOUIS VUITTON
MALLETIER A PARIS

MAISON FONDÉE EN 1854

BEYOND HOURS AND MINUTES
HISTORY IN TIME

Planetarium Copernicus, handmade in 18 ct gold, individually numbered, sapphire crystal, water resistant to 30 m, shockproof.

PLANETARIUM COPERNICUS

The Planetarium by Ulysse Nardin combines with a pure stroke of genius the geocentric universe with the Earth at the center of our solar system with the true astronomic heliocentric system with the Sun at its center. The classic planets Mercury, Venus, Mars, Jupiter and Saturn rotate around the Sun at their correct speed. The Moon rotates around the Earth. All planet cycles are synchronised and driven by an ingenious automatic movement. The Planetarium Copernicus can be reset forwards and backwards to any given date.

The Planetarium indicates:
- astronomical positions of the Sun, Moon and the planets Mercury, Venus, Mars, Jupiter, Saturn
- astrological positions of the Sun, Moon and planets
- ruling sign of the zodiac
- moon phases
- month
- date
- exact time

Mechanical Chronometers
and other complicated watches
since 1846

For further informations contact:
ULYSSE NARDIN SA, 2400 Le Locle CH, Tel. 0041 39 31 56 77, Tlx 952 346, Fax 0041 39 31 56 91 or BALTIC JEWELS, 39 Greville Street, LONDON ECIN 8PJ, Tel. 01 405 4623.
LONDON: Garrards, Mappin & Webb.

ZUERICH + AIRPORT: Türler; GENEVA: Masis, Moussaieff; LUGANO: Mersmann; MILANO: Società Astrolabio; ROMA: Hausmann; GERMANY: Wempe; NEW YORK: Tourneau; NEWPORT: Moboco; PALM BEACH: Embassy Watch; AMSTERDAM: Elka Watch; FUENGIROLA: Oro y hora; MADRID: Suarez; BARCELONA: San Gil; BANGKOK: Lotus Regent Hotel; HONG KONG: Dickson, Peninsula Hotel + Landmark; SINGAPORE: The Hour Glass; TOKYO: Bronica Trading; AUSTRALIA: Watch Gallery.

Christie's Country House Sales. The Glittering Prices of '88.

Last year, Christie's sold the contents of eight country houses realising an unprecedented £6½ million total.

Just as important as the money achieved, however, with all its background of professionalism and international marketing skills, are the tact and sensitivity that are called for when dealing with family possessions, often acquired over generations.

This is something we pride ourselves upon at Christie's. And perhaps indicates why we are already anticipating a record number of clients in 1989.

Please contact Elizabeth Lane on (01) 839 9060 for further information.

8 King Street, St. James's, London SW1Y 6QT
Tel: (01) 839 9060
85 Old Brompton Road, London SW7 3LD
Tel: (01) 581 7611
164-166 Bath Street, Glasgow G2 4TG
Tel: (041) 332 8134

CHRISTIE'S
COUNTRY HOUSE SALES

~ Bureau de Londres ~
L'Union des
Assurances de Paris

~ Established 1973 ~
Fondée 1828

THE SENSUAL PLEASURES OF BATHING

Imagine the pleasure of your perfume all around you, in the bath, softening your skin . . . in the air and through the day, with you, everywhere.

In Body Shampoo, Body Lotion, Body Creme, Talc, Deodorant, Bath Essence and Soap. From Shalimar to Bagatelle, Mitsouko to Chamade ~ abandon your body to the heady intoxication of your favourite perfume.

ÊTRE
GUERLAIN

GUERLAIN
PARIS

RED, WHITE AND ORANGE BOX.

"Ballerina" slippers. Agendas: red ostrich, blue lizard, white grained calf, white ostrich, red lizard, red crocodile. Pochette "Kelly". "Drum" bag.
Sac à Malice "Vive la France," "Kelly" bag. "Ex-Libris" scarves in cashmere and silk. "Flag" ties.
Silk carré "1789." Men's "Arceau" watch, steel plated gold. "Clipper" watch, steel plated gold. "Bucephale" bracelet GM in silver.

Please note: The watches shown in this advertising page are as such, available on the British market. However, and strictly for legal reasons concerning brand registration matters, this article cannot bear in this country the Hermès brand name.

HERMÈS
PARIS

It's got the largest back-up service in the aria.

The largest national paging network. The most extensive repertoire of pagers, portable and in-car Cellphones. The most critically acclaimed pre-sales equipment testing.

And to back it up, there's the biggest and most highly orchestrated customer care service in Britain. Staffed by a well-rehearsed cast of thousands.

There's even a free nationwide 'instant replacement' guarantee.

So you can be sure, whatever happens, we won't make a big number about sorting it out.

To find out more about the best supporting role in town, call our information line number below.

JUST CALL US FREE ON 0800 222 666

It's you we answer to

Virtuoso Performer

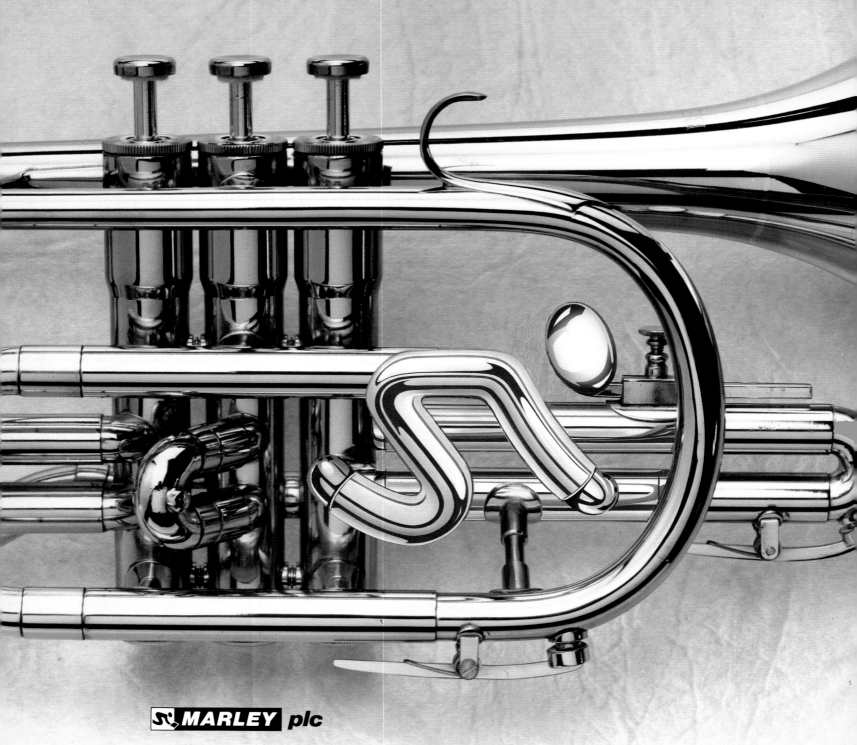

Taittinger.
Anything else is just champagne.

Fripp Sandeman
VERY SERIOUS RETAIL BUSINESS CONSULTANTS

Fripp Sandeman & Partners Limited, 2 Bedford Square, London WC1B 3RA. Telephone: (01) 834 8502.

Best Wishes to
Glyndebourne Festival Opera
1989

Rosehaugh Estates PLC

79 High Street, Eton, Windsor, Berkshire S24 1AF. Telephone: 0753 859010.

OPERA
FROM THE CLASSIC LABEL

Have you been to Marks & Spencer lately?

MARKS & SPENCER

THERE ARE OCCASIONS WHEN A WATCH BECOMES MORE THAN A TIMEPIECE. THE DUNHILL ELITE.

Everything that carries the Dunhill name has to be the best of its kind.
It has to have a lasting beauty and be both useful and dependable. To this end the skills of the finest craftsmen are
used to work the most precious metals. Dunhill has become a hallmark not just of inherent
British values but of quality the world over.

The Dunhill Elite. Designed in 18ct gold and in steel, from a collection
that includes watches embellished with diamonds. Its slim elegance and unique design make it a classic
timepiece. The numerals on the white enamel dial have been applied individually by hand
as a signature of both time and the craftsman's skill.

Without his patrons, who'd have heard Mozart play?

As a child prodigy, Mozart was in great demand in the Courts of Europe. He received 'golden opinions' everywhere, but not enough money for the barest necessities.

Help was at hand when the Archbishop of Salzburg awarded Mozart an honorary appointment as 'maestro di capella'.

When the Archbishop died in 1772, his successor proved to be less interested in music. Mozart asked the new Archbishop for leave of absence for a concert tour but was refused. The Archbishop disapproved of 'that system of begging'.

Mozart eventually resigned his appointment and began a tour in Munich. He discovered however, that a musician of 21 could not make the same impression as an infant prodigy.

Mozart was awarded another appointment as 'Kammercompositor' to the Emperor with the meagre salary of 800 guilders. When the Emperor died in 1790, Mozart was left to eke out his existence with various commissions. He died in poverty on December 5, 1791.

Without his patrons, however small, we may never have heard of him or his music. Not even in the odd bar.

Even now, the arts need our support.

If this page goes a little way to supporting today's arts, we are pleased we can help.

British Gas

Join the circle.

J&B Rare Scotch Whisky

In Perfect Harmony

Horsted Place

Make your Glyndebourne experience an aria of excellence. Impeccable service performed in sumptuous surroundings – just minutes away.

Relax, refresh with a dip in our heated indoor pool, enjoy the gardens and croquet or challenge the tennis court.

Horsted Place offers everything to make your visit to Glyndebourne an especially memorable occasion – we will even prepare your picnic . . .

Accommodation from £95 including English breakfast.

GRANFEL

For reservations or more information:
Horsted Place Little Horsted Nr. Uckfield East Sussex TN22 5TS
Tel: (0825) 75581 Tlx: 95545 Fax: (0825) 75459

"Darling you haven't forgotten the opera glasses?"

Silver Champagne Cooler **£6625**
Silver Plate Candelabra **£473**
Silver Caviar Dish **£3065**
Silver 3 pce Octagonal Condiment Set **£1645**
Silver Napkin Ring **£56**
Silver Cheese Knife, Chippendale **£32.00** (plate **£15.40**)
Silver Tea Spoon, Chippendale **£29.50** (plate **£7.90**)
Royal Copenhagen 'Flora Danica' Side Plate **£244**
Baccarat for Garrard Champagne Flute **£133.95** each
Cashmere Rug **£518**
Opera Glasses in Black Mother of Pearl **£220**

BY APPOINTMENT TO
H M THE QUEEN
GOLDSMITHS & CROWN JEWELLERS
GARRARD & CO LTD
LONDON

BY APPOINTMENT TO
H M QUEEN ELIZABETH THE QUEEN MOTHER
JEWELLERS & SILVERSMITHS
GARRARD & CO LTD
LONDON

GARRARD

THE CROWN JEWELLERS

112 REGENT STREET · LONDON W1A 2JJ · TEL: 01-734 7020
YURAKUCHO SEIBU · TOKYO · TEL: (03) 286-0111

Ravel
Bizet
Verdi
Mozart
Puccini
Gershwin
Strauss
Bowring

Proud to be in such distinguished company

Recitativo Accompagnato

WATES BUILD WITH CARE

1260 LONDON ROAD · NORBURY · LONDON SW16 4EG
TELEPHONE 01-764 5000

Just a few of the stars to look out for during the long interval.

We're sure that you'll enjoy all the stars at this year's festival

Beecham

BEST WISHES FROM THE WORLD'S LEADING PERFORMER BEHIND THE SCENES.

Honeywell products, systems and services are to be found behind the scenes of all manner of commercial, industrial and domestic buildings in Britain.

We make literally thousands of devices which perform any number of vital functions, from controlling the central heating in your home to controlling and monitoring sophisticated automated manufacturing plants.

We also play a major role in sponsoring artistic and cultural events.

But we don't like to make a big drama of it.

Honeywell

HELPING YOU CONTROL YOUR WORLD

HONEYWELL LTD., CHARLES SQUARE, BRACKNELL, BERKSHIRE RG12 1EB. TEL: 0800 521121. EXT 9090.

A FINE
CRITIQUE

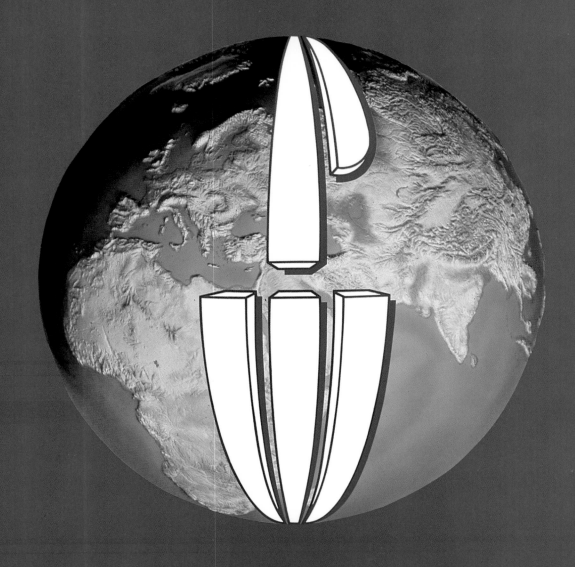

Price Waterhouse
Advising the world of business

Probably the best lager in the world.

This production is sponsored by the purveyors of Harveys Bristol Cream.

La Bottiglia Verde Scuro.

The scene is set in the neighbourhood of Bristol.

ACT I Scene 1   *Frederick's garrett.*

As the curtain rises, we find our hero, Frederick, alone in his draughty garrett, where he is struggling to complete his life's work – a musical involving the interwoven lives of the wildlife on the lonely Scottish island of Rhum. He is joined by his lover, Marie, the used-match seller. They sing a sad and haunting duet *('Oh for an arts council grant').* The unhappy couple then quarrel, Marie pointing out that the Capercallie has not nested on the island of Rhum for some 200 years. Frederick, mortified by his sweetheart's taunts, leaves.

ACT II Scene 1   *The street.*

We find Frederick wandering the streets, alone, until he happens upon a small off-licence. He enters, and is immediately captivated by Valentina, the shop-girl.

Scene 2   *In the Off-Licence.*

Valentina is a wild-haired gypsy girl of the kind often seen in the outlying districts of Bristol. Shunned by parents, friends and pets, she has come to the city centre to seek work. Dressed in her traditional blue checked nylon overall, she is as taken with the tall, dark potential customer as he is with her.

In a bid to win his heart, Valentina presses Frederick to a packet of cheese and onion crisps, but this crushes them and makes them difficult to eat.

Dinner interval of approximately 75 minutes.

ACT III Scene 1   *In the Off-Licence.*

We return to the off-licence, where as a last resort, Valentina opens a bottle of Harveys Bristol Cream. Frederick is immediately enchanted by its smooth, delicate taste and sings to his new-found sweetheart *('My love is like a dark-green bottle').* Valentina's brother, Marco, returns unexpectedly from overseas. The two sing a short, nostalgic ballad of their homeland in Tristan da Cunha. Marco leaves for overseas again.

Scene 2   *Frederick's garrett.*

Returning to his garrett, Frederick tells Maria of his intention to open a chain of off-licences with Valentina, and vows never to return. Alone now, Maria consoles herself by symbolically turning Frederick's masterwork into a collection of small origami animals, all the while singing a tragic aria *('The course of true love is rarely as smooth as the best sherry in the world').* The final curtain falls.

Opera at the time of the *other* Trafalgar.

(*Playbill of the world premiere of Fidelio, Beethoven's only opera.*)

Beethoven's only opera 'Fidelio' was first performed in 1805, the same year as the Battle of Trafalgar. The Trafalgar of today, Trafalgar House, is proud to extend its support and best wishes to the 55th birthday of the Glyndebourne Festival.

TRAFALGAR HOUSE
PUBLIC LIMITED COMPANY

FROM GLYNDEBOURNE TO YOUR DAUGHTER'S WEDDING, LETHEBY AND CHRISTOPHER ARE AT YOUR SERVICE.

Throughout the years of our association with Glyndebourne Festival Opera, the keynote of our service has always been gourmet food impeccably served.

Now, if you're planning a special celebration, we can put that same elegance and consistent high quality at your service.

Whether it's a wedding or grand formal event, a relaxed party or an important business occasion, we have both the highly trained staff and the years of expertise to make it truly memorable.

I'd like to discuss your needs personally. Call me, Peter Nichols, on 0273 812510.

LETHEBY & CHRISTOPHER

· PRIVATE CATERING ·

Glyndebourne Festival Opera, Lewes,

East Sussex. Tel (0273) 812510.

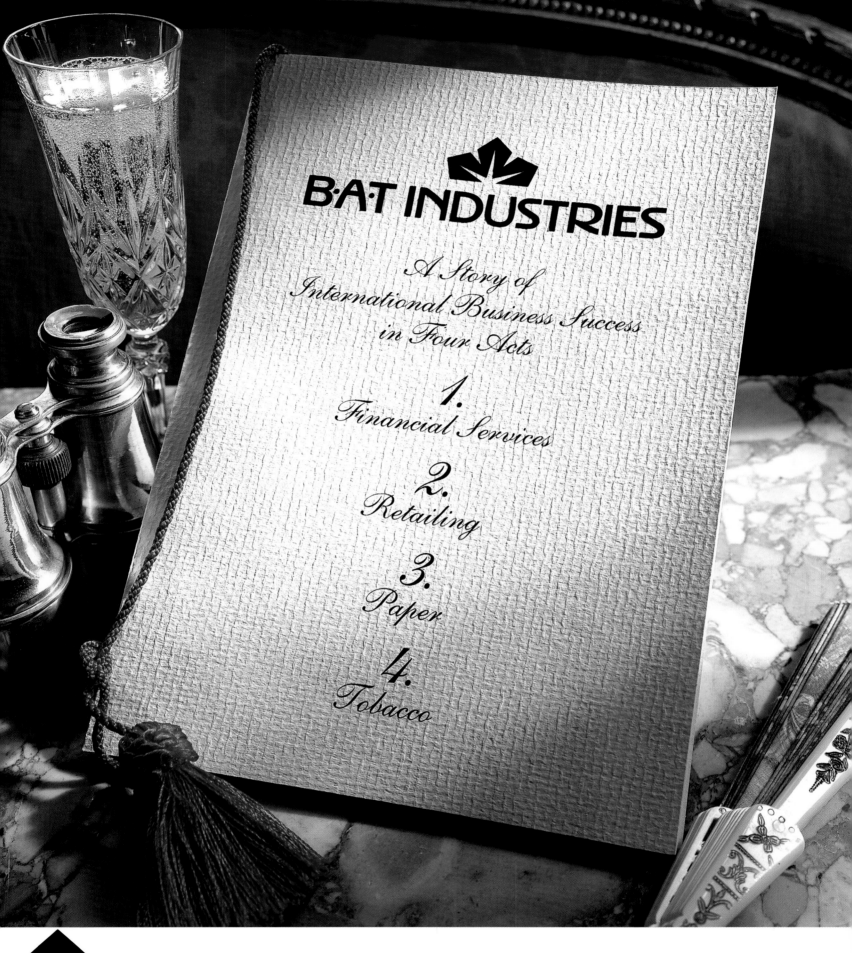

B·A·T INDUSTRIES

*A Story of
International Business Success
in Four Acts*

1.
Financial Services

2.
Retailing

3.
Paper

4.
Tobacco

**B·A·T INDUSTRIES**

WE DON'T CLING TO THE PAST. WE BUILD ON IT.

We Scots understand tradition. Style, as we see it, is timeless. Exceptional taste demands good design.

That's why such great care goes into every garment that carries the name of McGeorge. We use only the best grades of the

finest natural fibres, the rest just won't do.

Our exclusive colours and subtle designs are always in harmony with the latest fashions, yet at the same time

will express your very own personal taste. The quality of workmanship in every detail says

McGeorge before you ever see the label. There's just nothing like it in the world – but perhaps we're biased.

McGeorge OF SCOTLAND

**Cashmere from Scotland –
Quite simply – the Enjoyment of Excellence.**

MIDDLE TAR As defined by H.M. Government
Warning: SMOKING CAN CAUSE HEART DISEASE
Health Departments' Chief Medical Officers

Perfectly tuned – for a perfect performance

Amdahl – large-scale systems and services
for large-scale organisations

amdahl

Amdahl (U.K.) Limited, Viking House, 29-31 Lampton Road, Hounslow, Middlesex TW3 1JD. Telephone: 01-572 7383

PART OF THE SCENERY

STRUTT & PARKER

PROPERTY ADVISERS TO THE GLYNDEBOURNE ESTATE

13 HILL STREET, BERKELEY SQUARE, LONDON W1X 8DL. TELEPHONE 01- 629 7282

CANTERBURY CHELMSFORD CHELTENHAM CHESTER EDINBURGH EXETER GRANTHAM HARROGATE IPSWICH LEWES MOLD
MORETON-IN-MARSH NEWBURY NORWICH ST ALBANS SOUTH MOLTON SALISBURY TAUNTON TAVISTOCK

CREATION

FAY GODWIN

PEOPLE

ENVIRONMENTS

SOLUTIONS

Britain's most complete answer to the
needs of modern office planning
and interior furnishing.

GORDON RUSSELL

GORDON RUSSELL PLC, National Showroom and Sales Office, 44/46 Eagle St, London WC1R 4AP. Telephone: 01-831 0031.

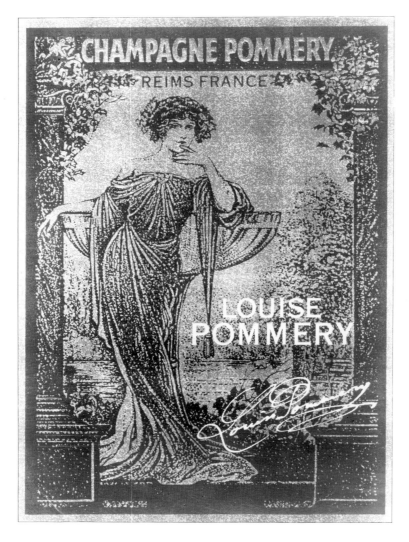

MAY THE ELEGANCE OF

YOUR EVENING MATCH THE

ELEGANCE OF

CHAMPAGNE POMMERY

BALLY

Who would have thought
computers had a part to play in opera?

"I think, therefore IBM."

GLYNDEBOURNE
Festival Opera

GERSHWIN

PORGY
AND
BESS

WILLARD WHITE · CYNTHIA HAYMON
AND **DAMON EVANS** AS **SPORTING LIFE**

OLYN BLACKWELL · BRUCE HUBBARD · CYNTHIA CLAREY · MARIETTA SIMPSON · GREGG BAKER
THE GLYNDEBOURNE CHORUS · THE LONDON PHILHARMONIC

SIMON RATTLE

EMI

DIGITAL

LP: PORGY 1 · CASSETTE: TCPORGY 1 · CD: CDPORGY 1

J M W Turner *A Lady in a Black Dress at her Toilet*   Reproduced by kind permission of the Trustees of the Tate Gallery

Westerham Press

Fine Art and Financial Printers

Printer of the Glyndebourne Festival Programme Book

London Road, Westerham, Kent, TN16 1BX
Telephone Westerham (0959) 63431

ORCHESTRA OF THE AGE OF ENLIGHTENMENT

Alex von Koettlitz

Violins
Roy Goodman *(Leader)*
Pavlo Beznosiuk *(Principal II)*
Sarah Bealby-Wright
Alison Bury
Susan Carpenter-Jacobs
Margaret Faultless
Desmond Heath
Rachel Isserlis
Stephen Jones
Sue Kinnersley
Peter Lissauer
Andrew Manze
Roy Mowatt
Pauline Nobes
Frances Turner
Henrietta Wayne
Catherine Weiss
Hildborg Williams

Violas
Jan Schlapp
Nicola Cleminson
Lisa Cochrane
Annette Isserlis
Martin Kelly
Nicholas Logie

Cellos
Angela East
Julie Lehwalder
Timothy Mason
Christopher Poffley
Richard Tunnicliffe
Helen Verney

Double Basses
Chi-chi Nwanoku
Ian Anderson
Judith Evans
Caroline Maguire

Flutes
Lisa Beznosiuk
Neil McLaren

Oboes
Anthony Robson
Richard Earle

Clarinets
Colin Lawson
Michael Harris

Bassoons
Andrew Watts
Frances Eustace

Horns
Susan Dent
Colin Horton

Trumpets
Mark Bennett
James Ghigi

Timpani
Janos Keszei

Harpsichord
John Toll

General Manager
Felix Warnock

Assistant Manager
Lesley Booth

Personnel Manager
Carole Becker

The Orchestra of the Age of Enlightenment has enjoyed spectacular popular and critical acclaim since its inaugural concerts in 1986 and has set new standards in the performance of baroque and classical music on instruments of the period.

The Orchestra has no principal conductor, which has enabled it to work with a brilliant succession of guest directors drawn from both the world of the Symphony Orchestra and Opera and from the more specialised field of period instrument performance.

Closely linked with an adventurous artistic policy has been the development of an enterprising sponsorship programme which has associated the orchestra in particular with Charterhouse plc principal sponsor for 1988 and 1989; with British and Commonwealth Holdings PLC who will also continue to support the Orchestra into the 1990s; with Bankers Trust Company who sponsored the London debut concert and who are supporting the orchestra in its perform-ances of Mozart's *Figaro* during this Glyndebourne season.

With a unique combination of scholarship and musical enthusiasm the OAE aims to give the best possible performances of baroque and classical masterpieces in a style that would have been familiar to the composers them-selves and to lead the field in the presentation of imaginative and innovative concert programmes.

The London Philharmonic

Hidden in the Darkness

by Richard Morrison

To the average music-lover on the Clapham omnibus – the passenger with the stereo walkman pumping Bartók or Bananarama into the cranium – an orchestra is just an orchestra. Musicians, however, know that orchestras come in as many delicate varieties as rare butterflies.

There are the world's great Philharmonics, as virtuosic as any soloist who may stand in front of them. There are the chamber orchestras who excel in close-knit teamwork. Sitting in subterranean darkness are the opera-house orchestras; they rise to epic musical challenges nightly while the tenors and sopranos collect the bouquets. Then there are the studio orchestras, painstakingly accurate for that most unforgiving of audiences: the microphone. You can also find 'pops' orchestras, baroque orchestras, and the brave orchestras which specialise in the agony and ecstacy of contemporary music.

One could go on, but you've got an opera to catch. In any case, an orchestra like the London Philharmonic transcends labels. It is one of the world's great Philharmonics, residing during the winter months at the Royal Festival Hall in the illustrious company of such maestros as Solti, Haitink, Tennstedt, Masur, Muti, Mehta and Rattle. Yet it is also one of the most recorded of all orchestras; and it can tackle new music as skilfully as the specialists, as last December's performances of Olivier Messiaen's gigantic music-drama *St Francis of Assisi* showed.

What makes it unique, however, is the three months each summer when it decamps to Sussex and transforms itself into an opera orchestra – Glyndebourne's orchestra. For players accustomed to being 'centre stage' themselves the anonymity of the theatre pit is refreshing, though there are different pressures. Instead of the urgent mastering of new repertoire each day, there are comparatively leisurely preparation periods. But then comes the commitment to maintaining top quality through perhaps 15 performances of the same work.

Undoubtedly the quarter-century association with this most artistically scrupulous of opera festivals has helped to mould the quintessential London Philharmonic 'sound'; equally, the quality of the sounds emerging from the pit has become an essential aspect of Glyndebourne's ethos of excellence. So enjoy the opera, and remember those extraordinarily talented people sitting hidden in the darkness. Yes, the music critics. But there is also a superb orchestra here.

Richard Morrison is a music critic on The Times

First Violins
David Nolan *Leader*
Stephen Bryant *Co-Leader*
Robert St. John Wright
John Kitchen
Sylvain Vasseur
George Apel
Penelope Wayne
Geoffrey Lynn
Thomas Eisner
Robert Pool
Maire Dillon
Cindy Foster
Russell Gilbert
Bjorn Petersen
Katherine Loynes
Susan Johnson

Second Violins
Dermot Crehan *Principal*
Geoffrey Price
Joseph Maher
Geoffrey Illman
Kenneth Weston
David Marcou
David McLaren
Brian Porter
Jennifer Nickson
Peter Mayes
Eleanor St George
Francesca Smith
Gillian Habgood

Violas
Norbert Blume *Principal*
Anthony Byrne *Co-Principal*
Stephen Broom
Julian Shaw
David Godsell
Robert Duncan
Roger Hall
James Brown
Josephine St Leon
Wrayburn Glasspool

Cellos
Robert Truman *Principal*
Matthias Feile *Co-Principal*
Francis Bucknall
John Lowdell
Santiago Sabino Carvalho*
Ronald Calder
Alexander Cameron
Roger Lunn

The London Philharmonic with its Conductor Laureate, Klaus Tennstedt, photographed in Regent's Park, London

Barry Lewis/Sunday Express Magazine

Basses
William Webster *Principal*
Kenneth Goode *Co-Principal*
Bryan Scott
Laurence Lovelle
David James
George Peniston

Flutes
Jonathan Snowden *Principal*
Celia Chambers *Principal*
Robin Chapman
Simon Channing
Lenore Smith

Piccolos
Jonathan Snowden
Celia Chambers
Robin Chapman

Oboes
Gordon Hunt *Principal*
David Cowley *Guest Principal*
Angela Tennick
Joan Whiting
Victoria Wood
Elizabeth Fyfe
Nicholas Winfield

Cors Anglais
Gordon Hunt
Joan Whiting
Nicholas Winfield
Elizabeth Fyfe

Clarinets
Robert Hill *Principal*
Roy Jowitt *Guest Principal*
Peter Maunder
Stephen Trier
Nicholas Carpenter

C Clarinet
Timothy Payne

Bass Clarinet
Stephen Trier

Basset Horn
Stephen Trier

Bassoons
John Price *Principal*
Philip Tarlton *Guest Principal*
Michael Boyle
Gordon Laing

Contra Bassoon
Gordon Laing

Horns
Nicholas Busch *Principal*
Richard Bissill *Principal*
Gareth Mollison
Frank Rycroft
Iain Keddie
Stephen Bell

Trumpets
Lawrence Evans *Principal*
Stanley Woods *Co-Principal*
Denis Curlett

D Trumpet
Lawrence Evans

Cornetti
Michael Laird
Jeremy West
Wendy Evans

Trombones
Michael Hext *Principal*
Colin Busby
Peter Harvey

Tuba
Owen Slade *Principal*

Timpani
Russell Jordan *Principal*
Neil Percy
Jeremy Cornes

Percussion
Keith Millar *Principal*
Jeremy Cornes
Peter Chrippes

Harps
Caryl Thomas *Guest Principal*
Janice Beven

* Chevalier of the Brazilian
Order of Rio Branco

**Administrator for the
London Philharmonic at
Glyndebourne**
Jacqueline Noltingk

Personnel Director
John Cobb

Registered offices
London Philharmonic
Orchestra Ltd
35 Doughty Street
London WC1N 2AA

Telephone: 01-833 2744
Telex: 8956666LPORCH
Fax: 01-837 1224

GLYNDEBOURNE
Festival Opera
1989

Founded in 1934 by Audrey and John Christie

General Administrator: Anthony Whitworth-Jones   Musical Director: Andrew Davis   Artistic Director: Sir Peter Hall CBE

Conductors:
Andrew Davis
Sylvain Cambreling
Jane Glover
Graeme Jenkins
Hermann Michael
Simon Rattle
Ivor Bolton

Head of Music Staff:
Martin Isepp

Senior Coaches:
Jonathan Hinden
Jean Mallandaine
Craig Rutenberg

Chorus Masters:
Ivor Bolton
David Angus

Language Coaches:
Ilya Bohac (Czech)
Rosetta Ely (Italian)
Gabriella Ezra (Italian)
Geraldine Frank (German)
Ernesta Partilora (Italian)

Music Staff:
Nancy Cooley
Joyce Fieldsend
Tom Gligoroff
David Gowland
James Holmes
Brenda Hurley
Steven Naylor
Mark Packwood
John Toll

Librarian:
Sarah Plummer
Associate: Charmian Hughes
Assistant: Gillian Brierley

Directors:
Peter Hall
John Cox
Nikolaus Lehnhoff
Michael McCaffery

Principal Associate Director:
Stephen Lawless

Revival Director:
Monique Wagemakers

Associate Directors:
Christopher Newell
Dagmar Thole

Staff Directors:
David Edwards
Michael Fry
Stephen Medcalf
Caroline Sharman
Robin Tebbutt

Designers:
John Bury
John Gunter
David Hockney
Tobias Hoheisel
Julia Trevelyan Oman

Choreographers:
Monique Wagemakers
Jenny Weston

Lighting Designers:
Robert Bryan
John Bury
Wolfgang Göbbel
Paul Pyant

Hon Electronic Engineering
Consultant: John Barnes

Casting Manager:
Felicity Jackson

Company Co-ordinator:
Jonathan Reekie

Assistant to the Opera
Manager:
Kathy Wolfenden

Auditions Secretary:
Helen Robbins

Technical & Production
Administrator: Tom Redman

Production Managers:
James Baird
David Locker

Personal Assistant to Tom
Redman: Carmel Gregg

Stage Managers:
Julie Crocker
Nicholas Murray

Deputy Stage Managers:
Helen McCarthy
Philip Ticehurst

Assistant Stage Managers:
Paul Bailie
Sarah Cotter
Catherine Hartley
Kathryn Hoodless
Gary Sparkes

Master Carpenter:
Ivor Green
Deputy: Andrew Vivian

Lighting Manager:
Keith Benson
Deputy: Mark Jonathan

Chief Electrical Technician:
Paul Hanrahan

Wardrobe Manager:
Tony Ledell
Deputy: Pamela McIntyre

Chief Cutters:
Jean Hunnisett (Wardrobe)
Sylvan Forde (Tailoring)

Wardrobe Mistress:
Ruth Featherstone
Deputy: Kate Vaughan

Wig Manager:
Barbara Burrows
Deputy: Gina Cyganik

Make-up Manager:
Celia Baxter

Property Manager:
Annabelle Hawtrey
Deputy: Vigee Harding

Financial & Commercial
Director: Mark Beddy

Treasurer:
John Barden

Assistant Treasurer:
Adrian Wines
Assistants: Ken Watkins,
Bernice Harvey, Diana
Durell

Administration Manager:
Shirley Honer

House Manager:
Geoffrey Gilbertson

Accommodation Manager:
Sheila Purbrook

Secretary to the Chairman:
Morwenna Brewer

Secretary to the General
Administrator:
Alison Chapman

Secretary to the House and
Accommodation Managers:
Amanda Blunden

Chief Telephonist:
Brenda Hermitage

Transport Officer:
Rosemary Martin
Associates:
Desmond Worsfold
Frank Waters

Head Gardener:
Chris Hughes

Press Secretary:
Joanna Townsend

Information and Sales:
Pat Walker
Sheila Hamilton

Archivist and Gallery
Manager: Rosy Runciman

Merchandise Manager:
Lari Powell

Marketing Manager, GTO:
Nicky Webb

Education Organiser:
Katie Tearle
Assistant: Tessa Chisholm

Festival Society Assistant
Secretary: Julia Watkins

Appointed Photographer:
Guy Gravett

Head of Press and Public
Relations:
Helen O'Neill
Ringmer (0273) 812321 or
01 731 3648

Box Office Manager:
Lesley Stansfield

Assistant Manager:
Janet Boyes

Glyndebourne Lewes
East Sussex BN8 5UU
Ringmer (0273) 541111

Catering under the direction of Letheby & Christopher Ltd   General Manager: Sean Hall-Smith Ringmer (0273) 812510

ALLIED·LYONS

A L L I E D - L Y O N S

generously sponsors
the new production of

Jenůfa

This is the company's first
sponsorship of a new production
at Glyndebourne, following
many years of patronage here.
Jenůfa is also a 'first' for Glyndebourne.
The production will be recorded
by TVS for later transmission
on Channel 4 and video release.

JENŮFA

ACT I *A lonely mill. Late afternoon*

Jenůfa is expecting a child by her cousin Števa, owner of the mill. In the company of Števa's jealous half-brother, Laca, and their grandmother (old Mrs Buryja), Jenůfa is anxiously awaiting Števa's return from the army recruitment board: if Števa has not been conscripted, they will be able to marry at once, without revealing Jenůfa's guilty secret.

The herd-boy, Jano, gleefully announces that Jenůfa has taught him to read. Old Mrs Buryja praises her grand-daughter's intelligence and common sense; Jenůfa replies that her common sense has long since 'flowed away like water'. Laca is trying to carve a whipstock but complains that his knife is blunt. The mill foreman offers to sharpen it for him. Goaded beyond endurance by Laca's jealous taunts, Jenůfa goes into the house, leaving the two men to comment on what a fine sister-in-law she will make for Laca.

The foreman has heard that Števa has not been conscripted after all; Jenůfa's joy at the news is shared neither by Laca nor by her stepmother the Sextoness (Kostelnička). The new recruits arrive in high spirits, with Števa at their head. When Jenůfa accuses him of being drunk, he rounds on her: doesn't she realise she is addressing Števa Buryja, mill-owner, loved by all the girls? Look, he says, one of them has given him a posy of flowers. Števa orders the musicians to strike up Jenůfa's favourite song, and leads a riotous dance in honour of their forthcoming wedding.

The Kostelnička interrupts the revelry. If Jenůfa marries this spendthrift, she will spend the rest of her life scraping for pennies. The Buryja family are all alike, she says: her own late husband (Števa's uncle) was the same – a blond, handsome, drunken wastrel. She issues an ultimatum: if Števa can prove his good intentions by not getting drunk for a whole year, then she will consent to the marriage.

Jenůfa is horrified at this fateful delay. Števa tries to appease her by declaring that she is the prettiest of them all; he loves her 'rosy-apple cheeks'. Grandmother Buryja sends him away to sleep off his drunkenness. Laca taunts Jenůfa with the posy which Števa had received from one of his admirers; she declares that she will wear it with pride. Laca tries to kiss her, but she repulses him. Angrily, he slashes her cheek with his knife.

Dinner interval of approximately 75 minutes

ACT II *The Kostelnička's living-room. Five months later; winter*

Jenůfa has had her baby in secret; little Števa, now a week old, is asleep in the next room. The Kostelnička tells Jenůfa she should pray to God that the baby will die and save the family from dishonour. She gives Jenůfa a sleeping-draught and sends her to bed.

Števa arrives, in response to a summons from the Kostelnička. He refuses to go in and look at his child, although he promises to pay for its upkeep. He cannot marry Jenůfa now: her face is disfigured, and she has become 'cross and miserable' just like her stepmother. Anyway, he says, he is engaged to the Mayor's daughter, Karolka, and that will be the end of the matter. Jenůfa cries out in her sleep; Števa departs hastily, to avoid having to face her.

Laca is next to arrive. He knows nothing of the baby, believing that Jenůfa has been away; he has just seen Števa visiting the house, and takes this as a sign that Jenůfa has come back. He begs the Kostelnička to let him marry Jenůfa after all, but she breaks the news to him that Jenůfa has given birth to Števa's child. In desperation, she suddenly tells Laca that the child has died and Števa is to marry someone else. She sends him off to find out more about the wedding. Left alone, she comes to a terrible decision: with the child out of the way, her foster-daughter will be saved from shame and disgrace. She takes the baby from the sleeping Jenůfa and goes out to drown it in the mill-stream.

continued on page 100

JENŮFA

Její Pastorkyňa (Her Foster-daughter)

Opera in three Acts

Music by Leoš Janáček
Text by the composer founded on a story by Gabriela Preissová

By arrangement with Alfred A Kalmus Ltd (Universal Edition)
First performance of the Brno Version, edited by Charles Mackerras and John Tyrrell

In the original Czech with English supertitles

Conductor	Andrew Davis
Director	Nikolaus Lehnhoff
Associate Director	Dagmar Thole
Designer	Tobias Hoheisel
Lighting Designer	Wolfgang Göbbel

Cast

Grandmother Buryja, *owner of the mill*	Drahomíra Drobková
Laca Klemeň ⎞ *stepbrothers, Grandmother*	Philip Langridge
Števa Buryja ⎠ *Buryja's grandsons*	Mark Baker
Kostelnička Buryjovka, *Grandmother Buryja's daughter-in-law*	Anja Silja
Jenůfa, the Kostelnička's *foster-daughter*	Roberta Alexander
Foreman at the mill	Robert Poulton
The Mayor	Gordon Sandison
His wife	Linda Ormiston
Karolka, *their daughter*	Alison Hagley
A maid	Sarah Pring
Barena, *servant at the mill*	Menai Davies
Jano, *a shepherd boy*	Lynne Davies
Aunt	Deirdre Crowley

The London Philharmonic

Performances on May 19, 22, 26, 28, June 1, 3, 6, 10, 13, 17, 23, 25
Curtain up 5.50pm   Dinner Interval 6.50pm   Curtain down 9.50pm approximately   Sundays one hour earlier

First performed at the National Theatre, Brno, 21.I.1904
First performance at Glyndebourne, 19.V.1989

The audience is particularly asked to refrain from applauding until the end of a scene or aria
The taking of photographs and the use of recording equipment in the auditorium are forbidden

continued from page 98

Jenůfa wakes from her drugged sleep, wondering when Števa will come to see his son. She discovers that the baby is missing, but concludes that her stepmother has taken him to show him off to the workers at the mill. She prays to the Virgin Mary to protect her child. The Kostelnička returns and tells Jenůfa that she has been lying in a fever for two days, during which time the child has died. She tells her that she is now 'free'; Števa no longer wants to marry her, and she should consider the faithful Laca.

Laca himself now returns, and loses no time in asking Jenůfa to marry him. She declares that she has neither 'property, nor honour, nor love', but accepts. An icy gust of wind blows the window open; gripped by remorse, the Kostelnička sees 'the face of Death' looking in at her.

ACT III   *Two months later; spring*

In spite of the Kostelnička's increasingly nervous state, preparations are under way for Jenůfa's marriage to Laca. The Mayor and his wife come to pay their respects; the Mayor's wife expresses surprise that Jenůfa should 'dress like a widow' for her wedding. Laca tells Jenůfa that he has overcome his resentment for Števa and has invited him to the wedding with his bride-to-be, Karolka. The village girls sing a song to Jenůfa; Grandmother Buryja gives the couple her blessing.

The Kostelnička is about to bless them in her turn when the proceedings are interrupted by a commotion outside: the body of a baby has been discovered in the frozen mill-stream. From its clothes Jenůfa identifies the dead child as her own. The villagers assume she must have killed it herself, but the Kostelnička reveals the truth and recounts the grisly details of her crime. Appalled, Laca blames himself. Karolka calls off her marriage to Števa.

Jenůfa realises that her stepmother had acted unselfishly, believing that she was protecting Jenůfa's honour. Jenůfa calls upon the wedding guests to understand and forgive. She tells Laca that he is free to go, but he promises to stay by her side; moved by his devotion, Jenůfa feels that God has at last blessed their love.

Jonathan Burton

A NOTE ON THE SCORE USED IN THIS PERFORMANCE

Jenůfa was first performed in Brno in 1904. An adventurous work for a small provincial town, it achieved a moderate success and continued to be performed in Brno and on tours of the surrounding regions over the next decade. During this period Janáček made a number of small revisions, and many of these were included when its vocal score was published in Brno in 1908. The work, however, was not heard outside Moravia, largely because of personal antagonism between Janáček and Karel Kovařovic, music director of the well-to-do National Theatre in Prague, whose acceptance of the opera was the logical stepping-stone to performance abroad.

It was twelve years before Kovařovic took on the work, and then on condition that he revise the score. This was possibly to justify his original opposition, though it could be pointed out that Kovařovic was an inveterate reviser: Dvořák's opera *Dimitrij* is still given in Kovařovic's revision of 1912. Janáček accepted all Kovařovic's changes – he had very little option if he wanted to hear his opera performed outside Brno and he was now 62. *Jenůfa* was thus first heard in Prague in 1916 in Kovařovic's revision and reorchestration. Soon after, Universal Edition published a vocal score and full score of this version, and it was in this form that the work established its world-wide success. In later correspondence, however, Janáček made it clear that he regretted Kovařovic's interventions, and resented the implication that his orchestration was incompetent. He pointed to the fact that Otakar Ostrčil, Kovařovic's successor at the National Theatre in Prague, gave his next operatic premiere, *The Excursions of Mr Brouček*, without any modifications.

Kovařovic's version of *Jenůfa*, however, became the standard and until recently the only available version of the score. In the mid-1960s the Czech conductor František Jílek performed Janáček's original ending on Czech radio but the rehabilitation of Janáček's version was due largely to Sir Charles Mackerras. Over a number of productions and performances, culminating in the Paris production of 1981, Sir Charles began gradually to reintroduce details of the original orchestration. His version was recorded by Decca in 1982 and first used for a UK stage production by Welsh National Opera in its 1984 revival of the opera. The version given at Glyndebourne this season is a refinement, based on further research by Charles Mackerras and myself. It represents the first performances of a new score of the 'Brno version' (as distinct from the Kovařovic 'Prague version') which will be made available by the original publishers, Universal Edition.

The changes that will be most readily noticed are the jettisoning of Kovařovic's grandiose canonic finale in favour of Janáček's more sober version, and the frequent replacement of Kovařovic's horns by Janáček's more grainy trombones. Other changes affect the orchestration of the Act 2 prelude and of the Kostelnička's monologue, and differences in placing the dramatic chords that close this act. The xylophone solo with which the opera opens is an octave lower and its entry after Števa's exit towards the end of Act 1 is dramatically delayed, starting up abruptly and strikingly. In general the score loses the extra doublings and sustaining instruments added by Kovařovic. Individual lines will be clearer, more exposed; the balance a little more precarious. There are also a number of changes affecting the voice parts. The most striking change, however, is one that takes the score back to before Janáček's 1908 revisions – the reinstatement of the Kostelnička's 'explanation aria' of Act 1, discussed at the beginning of my article on page 121.

John Tyrrell

ORFEO ED EURIDICE

ACT I

In a silent grove, Orpheus and his friends lament the death of his beloved wife Euridice. The grove echoes with his plaintive cries as his companions complete their obsequies at Euridice's tomb. He begs them to leave him and calls out in increasing anguish at his new desolation and the prospect of a life in which he will never again see his wife.

Amor appears. Jove has heard Orfeo's lamentations and has decided to offer him the chance to reclaim Euridice as a reward for the extraordinary love which he has shown for her. The god, however, imposes one condition: that Orfeo should never look at Euridice, no matter how much she pleads with him, until they are safely back in the land of the present and the living. Amor persuades Orfeo that his special powers in music will enable him to conquer the underworld and the hero sets off in search of his lost wife.

ACT II

At the entrance to Hades, Orfeo is confronted by the Furies who try to stop his progress. He is merely a mortal and cannot dare to go where only heroes and gods have gone before him. Orfeo explains that his mission is to reclaim Euridice and affectingly tells the Furies of his profound grief, begging them to have pity on him and to feel whatever compassion they can. The fiends are moved by his music and let him through into the Valley of the Blessed Spirits.

Orfeo then finds himself in a place of supreme tranquility and beauty. Confident that his search is almost over, he goes to find Euridice. His wife then appears with her new companions and together they praise the serenity and joy of the Elysian Fields. Orfeo encounters them again and asks for Euridice to be returned to him. The Happy Shades give Euridice to her husband and together the couple set off for the mortal world, Orfeo carefully avoiding Euridice's gaze.

Dinner interval of approximately 75 minutes

ACT III

Orfeo and Euridice make their way through a rocky pass leading from the Elysian Fields. Euridice is wretched and confused at Orfeo's refusal to look at her. He tries to persuade her of his love but she is unconvinced. Why did he bring her from such happiness to treat her so cruelly? Has she become ugly and hateful to him? She pours out her feelings to him until, finally relenting, he turns to face her. The happiness that follows is brief and soon Euridice becomes faint and cold as Death reclaims her. Orfeo tries desperately to keep her alive but his attempts are in vain. Orfeo laments this second death and resolves to kill himself, the only way in which he can be united with his dead bride. Amor appears again to halt the suicide and to restore Euridice to life.

The scene changes to a Temple of Love and here Orfeo and Euridice celebrate the power of love to transcend all mortal barriers and to endure for ever.

Michael McCaffery

ORFEO
ED EURIDICE

Opera in tre atti di Raniere de' Calzabigi

Musica di Christoph Willibald von Gluck

In the original Italian

Production originally sponsored by
John Player & Sons

Conductors	Hermann Michael
	Ivor Bolton (24, 29 June)
Director	Michael McCaffery
Assistant Director	Robin Tebbutt
Design and Lighting	John Bury
Choreographer	Jenny Weston

Cast

Orfeo	Diana Montague
Euridice	Cynthia Haymon
Amor	Deborah Rees

Dancers: Richard Chance, Nelson Fernandez, Jenny O'Dwyer,
David Ruffin, Kathryn Turner, Donna Winwood

Harpsichord continuo	Martin Isepp
	Jonathan Hinden (23 & 27 May)

The London Philharmonic

Performances on May 20, 23, 27, 31, June 2, 4, 8, 11, 14, 18, 24, 29
Curtain up 6.10pm   Dinner Interval 7.35pm   Curtain down 9.50pm approximately   Sundays one hour earlier

First performed in Vienna, 5.X.1762
First performance at Glyndebourne, 19.VI.1947
First performance of this production at Glyndebourne, 27.VI.1982
The opening performance in this Festival will be the 26th by Glyndebourne Festival and Touring Opera

The audience is particularly asked to refrain from applauding until the end of a scene or aria
The taking of photographs and the use of recording equipment in the auditorium are forbidden

A MIDSUMMER NIGHT'S DREAM

The scene is set in a wood near Athens

ACT I *A wood*

Deepening twilight; the earth breathes. Puck, the messenger of Oberon, and four fairy-servants of Tytania watch with alarm the confrontation of master and mistress whose quarrel over Tytania's new Indian changeling boy has thrown all Nature into reverse. She refuses to part with the child, and Oberon plans a malicious revenge: by squeezing the juice of a certain flower on her sleeping eyes, he can make Tytania 'madly dote' on the first creature she sees after waking. Puck is sent to fetch the magic herb.

Hermia and Lysander arrive from the court of Duke Theseus where their love has been proscribed and Hermia instructed to marry Demetrius. Vowing eternal devotion to one another they go their way, followed at once on the scene by the pursuant Demetrius, himself pursued by Helena, who adores him but whom he cannot abide.

Puck returns with the flower. Oberon's sympathies are roused by Helena's unhappiness, and, after relishing the prospect of Tytania's humiliation, he commands Puck to take a little of the juice and use it on the 'Athenian youth', ie. Demetrius, so that he may return the lady's love. Puck's more or less innocent misapplication of the elixir is the motor of the plot.

The wood clears, and six rustics appear in search of a quiet place in which to rehearse the play they hope to perform at the wedding of Theseus and Hippolyta. Despite Bottom the weaver's desire to play all the leading roles, casting of *Pyramus and Thisbe* is effected, and each returns to the city and the conning of his part. Hermia and Lysander, by now thoroughly weary and lost, lie down to sleep, and Puck squeezes the juice on Lysander's eyes. Helena returns, wakes him out of fear, and, further distracted by the unexpected hazard of Lysander's love, again flees into the wood. Lysander follows. Hermia wakes from a nightmare, and, finding herself alone, sets off in search of Lysander. Tytania, preparing for the night, calls for a lullaby, slips into sleep and is anointed by Oberon himself.

ACT II *The wood as before*

Tytania's sweet slumber is darkened by the rustles and echoes of dreams and by the working of Oberon's spell. The rustics rehearse; Bottom, after the exertions of a particularly Thespian outburst, retires into the bushes where Puck, seizing a chance for further mischief, crowns him with an ass's head. Bottom's mates scatter in terror, but Tytania, awakened by the racket, is enchanted by Oberon's spell to succumb to Bottom's beauty and compels him to remain in the wood. She orders the fairies to entertain her new love; Bottom calls for music and, swiftly exhausted in an ecstasy of trivial pleasures and excitements, yawns himself to sleep in Tytania's arms.

Puck's confusion of the two Athenian youths is rectified by Oberon who now squeezes the juice on the sleeping Demetrius who duly awakes and declares a passion for Helena. Her fury at his change of tone leads to a quarrel between the two women, friends from childhood, and an angry quartet which exhausts the participants who run off in several directions. Puck fills the night air with mist, and contrives that all four lovers return one by one to the same spot and lie down next to their true partner without recognising them as they fall asleep. Lysander is given a second dose, and all will be well.

Dinner interval of approximately 75 minutes

---

continued on page 106

A MIDSUMMER NIGHT'S DREAM

Opera in three Acts

Music by Benjamin Britten
Libretto adapted from Shakespeare by Benjamin Britten and Peter Pears
Published by Boosey and Hawkes Music Publishers Ltd

In the original English

This production was sponsored in 1981 by
Commercial Union Assurance Company Plc

Conductor	Jane Glover
Director	Peter Hall
Associate Director	Christopher Newell
Design and Lighting	John Bury
Choreography	Jenny Weston, based on the original by Pauline Grant

Cast

Cobweb,	*Fairies*	Stephen Catling
Mustardseed,		Christopher Orchard
Peaseblossom,		Christopher Skillicorn
Moth,		Paul Vetch
Puck		Daniel John
Tytania, *Queen of the Fairies*		Elizabeth Gale
Oberon, *King of the Fairies*		Michael Chance
Lysander *in love with Hermia*		Ryland Davies
Demetrius		Jeffrey Black
Hermia, *in love with Lysander*		Cynthia Buchan
Helena, *in love with Demetrius*		Annegeer Stumphius
Quince, *a carpenter*		Roger Bryson
Snug, *a joiner*		Andrew Gallacher
Starveling, *a tailor*		John Hancorn
Flute, *a bellows-mender*		John Graham-Hall
Snout, *a tinker*		Adrian Thompson
Bottom, *a weaver*		Curt Appelgren
Theseus, *Duke of Athens*		Robert Hayward
Hippolyta, *Queen of the Amazons, betrothed to Theseus*		Susan Bickley

The London Philharmonic

Performances on June 9, 12, 16, 20, 27, July 1, 3, 8, 10, 13, 17, 23
Curtain up 5.50pm   Dinner Interval 7.45pm   Curtain down 10pm approximately   Sundays one hour earlier

First performed at the Aldeburgh Festival, 11.VI.1960
First performance at Glyndebourne, 21.VI.1981
The opening performance in this Festival will be the 37th by Glyndebourne Festival and Touring Opera

The audience is particularly asked to refrain from applauding until the end of a scene or aria
The taking of photographs and the use of recording equipment in the auditorium are forbidden

continued from page 104

ACT III *Early next morning*

A serene prelude describes the awakening and enlightenment about to overtake Tytania, Bottom and the lovers.
Oberon has acquired Tytania's changeling boy, and ten-
derly undoes the Queen's spell as day breaks and distant
horns announce the end of the royal hunt and the start of
the wedding. Oberon and Tytania slowly 'rock the ground'
in a dance of reconciliation. Hermia, Lysander, Helena and
Demetrius share each other's amazement and delight in
arriving at their true affections and take the good news to
the Duke. Bottom wakes last, and puzzles most concernedly
of all on the events of the night. The rustics' play is saved,
and their exuberant sextet leads into a brilliant march and
full-blooded transformation as the scene shifts from the
wood to the celebration of no fewer than three marriages at
the Duke's court.

Pyramus and Thisbe is performed before a company which
is much too excited to give it more than irreverent and
chattering attention, and the festivities end on the stroke of
midnight when Theseus, Hippolyta and the four lovers
retire. The fairies appear; Oberon and Tytania bless the
couples and shield the house from harm. Puck, as convention demands, sweeps up the dust of the day's work, and
commits the fate of the entertainment into the hands of the
spectators.

Michael Ratcliffe

Glyndebourne
has given 292 performances of

Le nozze di Figaro

since 1934,
but this new production,
which is generously sponsored by

WATERFORD Wedgwood

is only the fourth in Glyndebourne's history.
The production will be recorded
by BBC Television for
future transmission and video release,
and will form part of the
Glyndebourne Touring Opera's
repertoire this autumn.

LE NOZZE DI FIGARO

The opera is based on Beaumarchais' comedy Le Mariage de Figaro
and the action occupies a single day.
The scene is set in the neighbourhood of Seville

ACT I *A half-furnished room in Count Almaviva's palazzo. Morning*

It is the morning of the day of the marriage of Figaro, who is now in the Count's service, to Susanna, the Countess's maid. While Susanna is trying on a new hat, she discovers that Figaro is measuring the floor because the Count has allotted the room to the betrothed couple. He points out the convenience of its situation, for it opens out of the rooms of both the Countess and the Count. Susanna suggests that the Count's motives are ambiguous and explains that he is making ardent advances to her and hopes to profit by his *droit du seigneur* in spite of having promised to abandon it. Figaro becomes furiously jealous and, left alone, declares his resolve to turn the tables upon the Count.

He goes out, and a scene follows between Bartolo and Marcellina, his former housekeeper. Marcellina wishes to prevent Figaro's wedding and to marry him herself. He has signed a marriage-contract with her in order to obtain the loan of a large sum of money from her. Bartolo, who is anxious to pay off his old score against Figaro, promises to give her assistance in arguing her case, which will be decided by the Count. Bartolo leaves, followed by Marcellina who, on her way out, meets Susanna returning and has a bitter exchange of pleasantries with her.

Susanna is now joined by the page, Cherubino. He explains that the Count has ordered him out of the house for flirting with Barbarina, Susanna's cousin and daughter of Antonio the gardener. He begs Susanna to ask the Countess to intervene on his behalf and goes on to say that it is the Countess herself that he is really in love with, though he is in love with Susanna, too, and with Barbarina, and even with Marcellina – in fact, with every woman he sets eyes on.

He is interrupted by the entrance of the Count, and hides behind an armchair. The Count begins to make love to Susanna, but in turn is interrupted by the entrance of Basilio, the music-teacher. The Count also hides himself behind the chair, while Cherubino takes refuge in its seat and Susanna covers him with a cloak. Basilio talks to Susanna of Cherubino's passion for the Countess, whereupon the Count emerges angrily from his concealment and orders the immediate expulsion of Cherubino from the house. Susanna pleads that he is only an innocent boy, but the Count describes how he caught him the day before hiding under a table in Barbarina's room. He describes his lifting of the tablecloth with a gesture which lifts the cloak from the chair in which Cherubino is actually hiding. The discovery is embarrassing not only to Cherubino, but to the Count, who has been overheard making love to Susanna.

There is a fresh interruption caused by the arrival of Figaro and a number of peasants. They have come, at Figaro's instigation, to thank the Count for his abandonment of the *droit du seigneur* and to ask him to ratify it by putting a white veil over Susanna's head. The Count evasively postpones the ceremony until later in the day. Meanwhile, he announces his forgiveness of Cherubino, but gives him a commission in his regiment which he must take up immediately. Figaro congratulates Cherubino ironically and describes the perils and grandeurs of the military career upon which he is embarking.

ACT II *The Countess's boudoir. Mid-day*

The Countess, alone, prays to the god of love to bring back her husband's affection. She is joined by Susanna and by Figaro, who explains his plot for baffling the Count. A note is to be conveyed to him anonymously, which will allege that the Countess has an assignation with someone that night; this will stir up his jealousy. At the same time Susanna is to send him another note arranging to meet him also that night, in the garden; but her place is to be taken by

continued on page 110

108

LE NOZZE DI FIGARO

Opera buffa in quattro atti

Musica di W A Mozart
Poesia di Lorenzo da Ponte

In the original Italian

Conductor	Simon Rattle
Director	Peter Hall
Associate Director	Stephen Lawless
Designer	John Gunter
Lighting Designer	Paul Pyant
Choreographer	Jenny Weston

Cast

Figaro, *servant to Count Almaviva*	Dale Duesing
Susanna, *maid to the Countess*	Joan Rodgers
Bartolo, *a doctor*	François Loup
Marcellina, *his former housekeeper*	Felicity Palmer
Cherubino, *page to Count Almaviva*	Marianne Rorholm
Don Basilio, *a music teacher*	Mario Bolognesi
Count Almaviva	William Shimell
The Countess	Gunnel Bohman
Antonio, *gardener to the Count*	Donald Adams
Barbarina, *his daughter*	Alison Hagley
Don Curzio, *a notary*	John Graham-Hall
Bridesmaid	Eleanor Bennett

Harpsichord continuo John Toll
Jonathan Hinden (15 July)

The Orchestra of the Age of Enlightenment

Performances on July 2, 4, 7, 9, 11, 15, 22, 24, 27, 31, August 3, 5, 8, 10, 12, 14
Curtain up 5pm   Dinner Interval 6.50pm   Curtain down 9.55pm approximately   Sundays one hour earlier

First performed in Vienna, 1.V.1786
First performed at Glyndebourne, 28.V.1934
First performance of this production at Glyndebourne 2.VII.1989
The opening performance in this Festival will be the 293rd by Glyndebourne Festival and Touring Opera

The audience is particularly asked to refrain from applauding until the end of a scene or aria
The taking of photographs and the use of recording equipment in the auditorium are forbidden

continued from page 108

Cherubino (whom Figaro has hidden away) disguised as a girl. The Countess is then to surprise them together and the Count will be at their mercy. Figaro retires and immediately sends in Cherubino, who begins by singing the Countess a love-song of his own composition. Then, when the boudoir door has been safely locked, he is dressed up in some of Susanna's clothes. He shows the Countess the patent of the commission which the Count has just given him, and she remarks that they have forgotten to put a seal upon it.

Susanna goes out to fetch something from her own room, which adjoins the boudoir, and the Countess is left alone with Cherubino, who at once begins making love to her. At that moment the Count is heard, unexpectedly knocking at the locked door. Cherubino takes refuge in the Countess's dressing-room and the indignant Count is admitted. He has already been made suspicious by the receipt of Figaro's note, and the Countess, greatly embarrassed, assures him that she has only been trying on clothes with Susanna. Just then the noise of an overturned chair is heard from the dressing-room. At this moment Susanna returns unnoticed to the boudoir from her own room and conceals herself in order to watch events. The Count now angrily calls on Susanna, if it is she, to come out of the dressing-room and show herself. The Countess forbids her to do so, and at last the Count goes off to fetch tools to break open the door, taking the Countess with him and locking the doors behind him. Susanna now emerges from her hiding-place, and tells Cherubino to come out of the dressing-room. He escapes from the boudoir by jumping out of the window, and Susanna takes his place in the dressing-room. The Count and Countess return, the door of the dressing-room opens and Susanna steps out, to the relief of the Countess and the chagrin of the Count.

Figaro enters, to announce that preparations for the ceremony are complete and to obtain the Count's final approval. He is interrupted by the appearance of Antonio, the gardener, who has come to complain that the flower-beds have been damaged by someone jumping out of the window. The Count's suspicions are again roused, but Figaro saves the situation by declaring that he was the person responsible. Antonio thereupon produces a document which fell from the pocket of whoever it was who jumped out of the window. The Count, without letting Figaro see it, asks him what it is. Figaro is at a loss until, prompted by the Countess, he declares that it is the commission which Cherubino had handed to him in order to get it sealed. Once more the Count is baffled. Bartolo,

Basilio and Marcellina now rush in to demand the Count's judgement in favour of Marcellina's marriage-contract with Figaro; the Count postpones his decision and the scene closes with mutual recriminations between the two sets of antagonists.

Dinner interval of approximately 75 minutes

ACT III   *A hall in the palazzo. Afternoon*

On the Countess's orders, Susanna promises to meet the Count in the garden in the evening. The Count is delighted. As Susanna goes out she meets Figaro and boasts to him that she has won his lawsuit for him. The Count overhears her words and is overwhelmed with shame and rage.

The Countess reflects by herself upon the project of dressing in Susanna's clothes that evening and of herself keeping Susanna's assignation with the Count. She laments the need of such stratagems and looks back to a happier past and forward to a more hopeful future.

There enter Bartolo, Marcellina and Figaro, together with a lawyer, Don Curzio, who, with the Count's approval, gives a judgement that Figaro must either pay Marcellina his debt or marry her. In the nick of time, however, the fact emerges that Figaro is the illegitimate son of Marcellina and Bartolo. He embraces his newly-found mother, to the rage of Susanna (who comes in at that moment) until she learns the truth, and to the further discomfiture of the Count. At the Countess's dictation, Susanna writes a note to the Count, making a definite rendez-vous. She fastens it with a pin and asks for the pin back as a sign of assent.

The village girls come in with flowers for the Countess, among them Barbarina and Cherubino dressed as a girl. His disguise is exposed by Antonio, who enters with the Count; but the latter's anger is checked by Barbarina, who, with embarrassing naivety, reminds him of a former promise he had made to her and asks to be allowed to marry Cherubino. A procession is formed for the bridal festival of Figaro and Susanna.

The Count, with much ceremony, places a veil upon Susanna's head. As he does so, she slips the note into his hand and he pricks himself with the pin as he is reading it. Figaro notices the latter incident but not the origin of the note. The ceremony ends with an announcement by the Count of yet more celebrations.

ACT IV *The garden. Night*

Barbarina is searching in the darkness for something she has dropped. She innocently tells Figaro, who asks what she is looking for, that it is a pin that the Count has given her, to hand over to Susanna. Figaro guesses that an assignation is being made and elicits the details from Barbarina. While Figaro goes out raging against the apparent perfidy of Susanna, Barbarina conceals herself to await Cherubino. Figaro returns with Bartolo and Basilio and tells them to be at hand to witness the discomfiture of the Count which he is planning. Basilio deprecates such violent reactions and argues the advantages of adopting a metaphorical ass's skin as a defence against the dangers of life. Figaro, left alone, reflects upon the sufferings of married men and the monstrous wickedness of women. He retires for a moment, while the Countess and Susanna enter and exchange cloaks. The Countess withdraws and Susanna's thoughts, while she waits, turn to her lover.

The Countess enters once more, and is followed by Cherubino who threatens to spoil everyone's plans by making love to the pretended Susanna. At last the Count, waiting his chance in the background, drives off Cherubino. The Count now proceeds to make ardent love to the supposed Susanna, while the real Susanna and Figaro watch from a distance. At last Figaro interrupts them and the Countess goes off, followed by the Count. Figaro is joined, as he at first imagines, by the Countess and tells her how her husband is being unfaithful to her. Susanna (for it is really she) tries as a joke to get Figaro to make love to her; at first, still thinking he is talking to the Countess, he is taken aback, but quickly recognises Susanna by her voice and, without letting her see that he recognises her, falls in with her game. After a few moments Susanna abandons her pretence and the misunderstanding is put straight. Meanwhile, the Count, who has failed to follow the supposed Susanna, returns, and Figaro and Susanna repeat their comedy for his benefit. Furious with jealousy at the apparent sight of Figaro making love to his wife, he gives the alarm and denounces the two malefactors. Everyone in succession implores him to have mercy, but he remains obdurate. Suddenly, the Countess herself emerges from the shadow to add her voice to the suppliants. The Count, with his own infidelity and hypocrisy exposed, is overwhelmed with remorse and begs the Countess for forgiveness. He receives her pardon and the day of intrigue and mischief is brought to a joyful end.

Based on a synopsis written in 1934 for Glyndebourne by the late
James Strachey

BANKERS TRUST COMPANY

provides sponsorship for

The Orchestra of the Age of Enlightenment's performances of

Le nozze di Figaro this summer.

Their support for a major musical innovation

at Glyndebourne is very gratefully acknowledged.

ARABELLA

The scene is set in a Vienna hotel in the 1860s

ACT I *The salon of the Waldners' apartment*

Countess Waldner, anxious about her husband's imminent bankruptcy, consults a fortune-teller. She pins all her hopes on a good marriage for her elder daughter, Arabella, a beautiful, distinguished girl who is not short of eligible suitors. Zdenka, her younger daughter, is meanwhile disguised as a boy to avoid the expense of suitably presenting two girls in Viennese society.

Matteo is a young officer, passionately in love with Arabella. She, however, does not love him. Zdenka, whom Matteo takes for Arabella's brother, protects him from the truth by forging letters from Arabella in order to keep his hope alive. Zdenka loves him herself, but in her masculine guise cannot confess it.

Arabella, returning from a walk, is fascinated by the image of a stranger she saw opposite the hotel.

Zdenka persistently urges Arabella to accept Matteo, until eventually Arabella explains that she cherishes within her an ideal of 'the right man'. For her, marriage is such a sacred state that compromise disgusts her.

Is it, perhaps, Elemer? He is a brilliant, dashing nobleman of great wealth and style who is currently the leading contender. Arabella flirts with him wittily but finally refuses to go sleighing with him unchaperoned.

Count Waldner reveals to his wife that he is flat broke. He had been hoping to hear from Mandryka, an old regimental comrade to whom he had written, enclosing a photograph of Arabella, hinting that she was available. Suddenly Mandryka is announced and Waldner is overjoyed; but in walks a total stranger. Old Mandryka is dead, and the visitor is his nephew and heir. He had fallen in love with a picture of Arabella, and has now come from distant Slavonia to see if she is still single. Waldner consents to their marriage, borrows a few thousand from his future son-in-law and returns at once to his gambling. Arabella, unaware of these events, fantasises about the stranger she saw that morning. She has been chosen as Carnival Queen, and she has resolved that tonight she must make her choice.

Short interval (approximately 25 minutes)

ACT II *The ante-room to the Ballroom*

Arabella and Mandryka meet for the first time at the Cabbies' Ball. To the chagrin of Arabella's three suitors, the two fall immediately in love. They exchange personal vows and describe their future life together in Slavonia. He tells her how, were they there now, she would, by custom, bring him a glass of clear water from the well as a token of their troth.

However, Arabella is aware of her obligations as the Carnival Queen and asks Mandryka to leave her among her friends to bid farewell to her girlhood. He says that his place is near her; but she has his leave to ignore him for the rest of the evening.

At this point the three suitors lead the entire company in to crown Arabella as Carnival Queen. After the ceremony, dominated by Fiakermilli, the Cabbies' 'mascot', Arabella leads everyone back to the ballroom.

Mandryka informs the ecstatic Waldners that Arabella has accepted him, and orders a celebratory supper for them, with champagne for the entire company. Then Arabella takes leave for the last time of the three suitors who have been closest to her. Matteo finds Arabella's radiance bitterly painful, since it is not directed at him. Zdenka sees his desperation and urges him to accept an envelope from her. It contains, she says, the key to Arabella's room. He is

Continued on page 114

112

ARABELLA

Lyrische Komödie in drei Aufzügen Hugo von Hofmannsthal
Musik von Richard Strauss

Published by Boosey & Hawkes Music Publishers Ltd

In the original German

This production was sponsored in 1984 by
John Player & Sons

Conductor	Graeme Jenkins
Original Director	John Cox
Revival Director & Choreographer	Monique Wagemakers
Designer	Julia Trevelyan Oman
Lighting Designer	Robert Bryan

Cast

A fortune-teller	Enid Hartle
Adelaide, *wife of Graf Waldner*	Elisabeth Glauser
Graf Waldner, *a retired army Captain*	Ernst Gutstein
Zdenka } *their daughters*	Harolyn Blackwell
Arabella }	Felicity Lott
Matteo, *an officer*	David Kuebler
Mandryka	Sergei Leiferkus
Graf Elemer }	Kim Begley
Graf Dominik } *admirers of Arabella*	Gerald Finley
Graf Lamoral }	Alastair Miles
Die Fiakermilli	Sunny Joy Langton

Waiter: Andrew Yeats

Servants: Jonathan Veira (Welko), Robert Gibbs (Djura), Jozik Koc (Jankel)

The London Philharmonic

Performances on July 16, 21, 25, 29, August 2, 6, 9, 13, 16, 18, 20, 22
Curtain up 5.25pm   Dinner Interval 7.45pm   Curtain down 9.55pm approximately   Sundays one hour earlier

First performed in Dresden, 1.VII.1933
First performance at Glyndebourne, 7.VII.1984
The opening performance in this Festival will be the 27th by Glyndebourne Festival Opera

The audience is particularly asked to refrain from applauding until the end of a scene or aria
The taking of photographs and the use of recording equipment in the auditorium are forbidden

Continued from page 112

to leave the ball immediately to go to her, where she will grant all he desires.

Unfortunately, this scene is witnessed by Mandryka, who is stung into a fury of disbelief, jealousy and humiliation. His servants fail to find Arabella in the ballroom, and his suspicions seem to be confirmed when one of them brings a note from Arabella saying she has left early and looks forward to seeing him tomorrow. At this, his self-control breaks down completely as he coarsely toasts Fiakermilli. Eventually Countess Waldner intervenes, and when Mandryka insults her, she sends for her husband. He insists that Mandryka accompany them home to seek out the truth. Mandryka's parting shot is to invite the Viennese he so bitterly despises to drink all his champagne, and it is left to Fiakermilli to rescue the party.

Dinner interval of approximately 75 minutes

ACT III *The hotel lobby*

The key was in fact to Zdenka's room, not to Arabella's, and Matteo emerges thinking that it is to Arabella he has been making love. His amazement at finding her a few minutes later, fully dressed in the hotel foyer, is quickly superseded by frustration and rage at her complete lack of tenderness toward him. The Waldners and Mandryka return from the ball. In spite of Arabella's denial, Mandryka is convinced of her guilt, and matters deteriorate when Matteo attempts to protect her. Finally, since Arabella refuses to satisfy the question of honour by agreeing to marry Matteo, Mandryka agrees to a duel.

Suddenly Zdenka, no longer disguised as a boy, rushes downstairs in terror and confesses all. Mandryka begs forgiveness of Arabella and in a great outburst of generous feeling asks Waldner to give Zdenka to Matteo. As the family retire, Mandryka remains in the darkened foyer cursing his failure to trust Arabella. His heavy heart is lightened when Arabella emerges from her room and, in traditional Slavonian manner, brings him a glass of water to set the seal of their betrothal.

John Cox

EA

ENGLISH & AMERICAN GROUP PLC

sponsor the revival of this
celebrated production of

The Rake's Progress

This is English & American's first
major sponsorship in opera,
and marks the 60th anniversary
of its subsidiary,
English & American Insurance Company,
which was formed in 1929.

THE RAKE'S PROGRESS

ACT I Scene 1 *The garden of Trulove's house in the country. Spring*

Tom Rakewell, a young and impecunious country gentleman, is in love with Anne Trulove, but her father the squire, though anxious for their happiness, secretly doubts Tom's strength of character. He feels that his suspicions are confirmed when Tom refuses his offer of steady employment in the City. Tom is content to put his trust in Fortune. A stranger, who announces himself as Nick Shadow, suddenly arrives with the news that an unknown uncle of Tom's has died and left him a fortune. Tom must go at once to London to wind up his uncle's estate and Shadow offers himself as Tom's servant and guide through the intricacies of London life. The question of his salary can be decided in due course – a year and a day thence. Tom shall pay him what his services prove to have been worth. Tom takes leave of Anne and her father and sets off with Shadow for London.

Scene 2 *Mother Goose's Brothel, London*

Shadow introduces Tom to the opportunities bestowed by his new-found wealth. With whores and roaring-boys as an appreciative audience, Tom repeats the catechism of his new creed to Mother Goose, who presides as Lady Bishop in the ceremony of initiation. His responses are correct until a question about the meaning of love revives memories of Anne and his former happiness. Mother Goose persuades him to drink more deeply and his remorse vanishes. The whores offer to help banish his sadness, but Mother Goose claims him as her own.

Scene 3 *Trulove's Garden. Winter*

Months have passed but Anne has heard no news of Tom. She senses that Tom needs her and resolves to go in search of him in London.

ACT II Scene 1 *The morning-room of Tom's house in a London square*

Tom is surfeited and bored by his life in London and seeks in vain for happiness. Shadow exhorts him to marry Baba the Turk, the new sensation of St Giles' Fair. Only if he acts freely can he be happy. To be free he must defy the tyranny of appetite and duty – the bearded Baba is the antithesis of appetite and he owes her no duty. She is therefore the perfect agent for his happiness. Tom allows himself to be persuaded by Shadow and sets off to woo and win her as his bride.

Scene 2 *The street in front of Tom's house*

Anne finds her way to Tom's house and sees him arrive home, escorting a closed sedan chair. She greets him, but he begs her to return home and forget him. London is no place for her goodness and virtue. Anne reaffirms her love for Tom but leaves him shamed when she learns that the impatient occupant of the sedan chair is Baba the Turk, now his wife. Tom leads the veiled Baba to the house. The townspeople crowd round the door begging for a glimpse of her and in response to their excited requests, she unveils.

Dinner interval of approximately 75 minutes

Continued on page 118

THE RAKE'S PROGRESS

Opera in three acts

Music by Igor Stravinsky
Libretto by W H Auden and Chester Kallman

Published by Boosey & Hawkes Music Publishers Ltd

In the original English

Conductor	Sylvain Cambreling
Director	John Cox
Assistant Director	David Edwards
Designer	David Hockney
Lighting Designer	Robert Bryan

Cast

Anne Trulove	Sylvia McNair
Tom Rakewell	David Rendall
Trulove, *Anne's father*	Peter Rose
Nick Shadow	Jeffrey Wells
Mother Goose	Linda Ormiston
Baba the Turk	Anne Howells
Sellem, *an auctioneer*	Alexander Oliver
The Keeper of the madhouse	Alastair Miles

Harpsichord played by Jonathan Hinden

The London Philharmonic

Performances on July 30, August 1, 4, 7, 11, 15, 17, 19, 21, 23
Curtain up 5.30pm   Dinner Interval 7pm   Curtain down 9.50pm approximately   Sundays one hour earlier

First performed in Venice, 11.IX.1951
First performed by Glyndebourne at the Edinburgh Festival, 25.VIII.1953
(first professional stage performance in Great Britain)
First performed at Glyndebourne, 20.VII.1955
First performance of this production at Glyndebourne 21.VI.1975
The opening performance in this Festival will be the 88th by Glyndebourne Festival and Touring Opera

The audience is particularly asked to refrain from applauding until the end of a scene or aria
The taking of photographs and the use of recording equipment in the auditorium are forbidden

Continued from page 116

Scene 3   *Tom's morning-room*

Baba sits at breakfast with Tom among the bric-à-brac of presents given to her on a series of triumphant European tours by her countless admirers. Tom is bored and infuriates her with his indifference. She accuses him of retaining his love for Anne and rages and screams her jealousy until Tom silences her. Then he relapses into sleep – the last refuge of the bored. Shadow now prepares to complete Tom's downfall by adding financial disaster to his moral and domestic ruin. He wheels in a fantastic bogus machine for converting stones into bread. Tom wakes and tells Shadow that he has been dreaming of just such a machine. He does not realise that it is bogus, but believes that it will cure poverty and bring happiness to the wretched. Thus with good deeds he may again be worthy of Anne's love. He leaves to devote all his energies to collecting money for this noble and philanthropic scheme.

ACT III Scene 1   *Tom's morning-room*

Tom's financial bubble has burst, bringing ruin to himself and to countless innocent investors in his scheme. A crowd of inquisitive townsfolk flocks to attend the auction of his belongings. Anne arrives to ask news of Tom, but no-one can tell her where to find him. The auctioneer, Sellem, begins to auction the contents of the house. The bidding is spirited, until he offers a mysterious object. It is Baba, who springs to the defence of her belongings, unconscious of the intervening time since Tom silenced her. Tom and Nick are heard singing from the street, mocking Baba. Anne returns at the sound of the voices. Baba tells her that it is Anne whom Tom still loves and that her love may still be able to save him. Anne rushes out to seek for Tom, and Baba determines to go back to her true profession, the stage.

Scene 2   *A churchyard*

A year and a day have passed since Shadow entered Tom's service. He now claims his wages, Tom's soul. An open grave is waiting. He first offers Tom a choice of death by poison, steel, rope or gun, and then proposes that they play cards to decide Tom's fate. Shadow attempts to cheat, but memories of Anne inspire Tom to win the game. Shadow is enraged at being outwitted, but though cheated of Tom's soul, takes his revenge by striking him with insanity.

Scene 3   *Bedlam*

Tom is confined among the lunatics in Bedlam. He thinks himself to be Adonis and when Anne comes to visit him, believes that she is Venus, whom he has long been seeking. He asks her forgiveness for so long disdaining her love. She comforts him and sings him to sleep with a lullaby. Her love is unaltered, but realising that it is Venus and not herself whom Tom now needs, she sadly agrees to return home with her father. Tom wakes to find Venus has gone and his heart breaks in despair. The lunatics join in mourning Adonis, Venus's beloved.

Epilogue

The principals join in pointing out the moral of the fable, that the Devil finds work for idle hands.

John Cox

The Glyndebourne Chorus 1989

Chorus Masters: Ivor Bolton
      David Angus (from 1 June)

Sopranos
Susan Arnold
Cheryl Barker
Linda Clemens
Sally Driscoll
Karen Hoyle
Heather Lorimer
Rosalind Martin
Gaynor Morgan
Penelope Randall-Davis
Elizabeth Rodger*
Sarah Pring*

Contraltos
Eleanor Bennett*
Jane Cammack
Helen Cannell
Gemma Carruthers
Louise Crane
Deirdre Crowley
Rachael Hallawell
Deborah Hawksley
Denise Hector
Alison Hudson
Tamara Mitchel

Tenors
Robert Carlin
Grant Crawley
David Dyer
Robert Gibbs
Christopher Lemmings
Duncan MacKenzie
Andrew MacKenzie-Wicks
Iain Paton
Stephen Rooke
Richard Sweden
Christopher Ventris*
Andrew Yeats

Basses
Michael Carlyle*
Nigel Cliffe
David Guest
Richard Halton
Aneirin Huws
Charles Kerry* (*Chorus Manager*)
Jozik Koc
John Oakley-Tucker
Martin Oxenham
Peter Snipp
Graham Stone
Jonathan Veira*

* These singers have appeared as soloists with Glyndebourne Touring Opera

Glyndebourne is grateful to the following administrations for the granting of leave of absence to artists taking part in the Festival:

Royal Opera House, Covent Garden
Kim Begley

Frankfurt Opera
Marianne Rorholm

Kirov Opera, Leningrad
Sergei Leiferkus

Royal Opera, Stockholm
Curt Appelgren

Welsh National Opera
Peter Rose

John Cox is Director of Production, **Royal Opera House, Covent Garden**

John Gunter is Head of Design at the **National Theatre, Great Britain**

Boys' Chorus in *A Midsummer Night's Dream* appear by kind permission of the Headmaster, **Trinity School, Shirley Park, Croydon,** Director of Music David Squibb

James Arneill
Raymond Dunlop
Justin Jones
Andrew Northcott
Thomas Pezier
Roger Simpson
Stuart Smith
Matthew Swan
Alexander Willson

Children appear by kind permission of the Headmasters, **South Malling CE School** and **Lewes Ringmer County Primary School**

Movement
A Midsummer Night's Dream
Sandra Arabian
Roy Ashby
Martin Garfield
Lorraine Gill
Roderick Hart
Caroline Jennings
Rosemary Jolliffe
Edgar Newman
Bryan Payne
Guy Picot
George Reid
David Turner

Technical Staff

Technical and Production Administrator: Tom Redman
Production Managers: James Baird, David Locker

Staff Carpenters:
Rex Carter
Frank Eade
Martin Sheriff

Head Flyman:
Andrew Loader
Deputy:
Robert Wilson

Production Electrics:
Greg Hamlin
Gary Hanrahan
Jason Hares
Paul Hastie

Stage Staff:
Matthew Cole
Russell Dean
Robert deBradeny
Paul Edlund
Stuart French
Richard Gosling
Marcus Harvey
James Hastings
Jonathan Light
Nicholas Mitchell
Adrian Peacock
Anthony Pike
Duncan Pratley
John Rolf
Edward Taylor
Fred Townsend
Jonathan Whitmore

Wardrobe
Assistant Cutters:
Sarah Cook
Janet Powell

Assistants:
Tracey Catterall
Gabrielle Hawtrey
Beryl Horsfield
Nicole Oblanski
Kathryn Turner

Tailoring
Assistant Cutters:
Joan Collom
Elizabeth Jones

Assistants:
Audrey Bernard
Deborah Jones
Kim Jones
Claire McDonald
Juliet Nichols
Kate Strachan

Chief Dresser:
Kay Chandler

Wigroom Assistants:
Janice Barnes
Audrey Farman
Alison Guy
Linda Martin
Carol Meddins
Christina Miller
Colleen Morrison
Samantha Smart
Anne Smith

Property Staff:
Rose Beale
Gail Maidment
Lynn Naysmith
Clive Ventris

Children's Chaperones:
Jean Exley
David Squibb

Scenery construction and painting for *Jenůfa* by Alastair Flint
Scenery construction for *Orfeo ed Euridice* by Victor Mara Ltd, painted by Harkers Studios and Victor Mara Ltd
Scenery construction and painting for *Le nozze di Figaro* by Victor Mara Ltd
Scenic designs for *A Midsummer Night's Dream, Arabella* and *The Rake's Progress* realised by Albert Pullen and constructed under his supervision by Kier (RBW) Ltd, and at Glyndebourne
Scenery painted by Harkers Studios under the supervision of Stephen Jetten
Costume designs realised by Tony Ledell
Costumes made by the Glyndebourne Opera Wardrobe under the supervision of Tony Ledell, and by Arthur Davey, Doreen Brown, Dennis Bruno, Carol Hersey and John King
Painting and Dyeing: Alex Carey
Hats, head-dresses and masks: Gerald Cheshire, Simon Daws and Martin Adams
Specialist embroidery by Phyllis Thorald
Jewellery: Mark Haddon
Feathers: Elsa Rule
Shoes by Anello & Davide and Savva

Costume cleaning by New Theatre and Opera Cleaners (UK) Ltd and Celebrity Cleaners, London
Footwear repaired by Cobblers, Lewes
Wig designs realised by Barbara Burrows
Wigs made in the Glyndebourne Wig Department under the supervision of Barbara Burrows
Property designs realised by Annabelle Hawtrey
Properties and Set Decorations made in the Glyndebourne Property Department under the supervision of Annabelle Hawtrey
Additional scenic properties for *Le nozze di Figaro* by Sarah Baker and Roger Cresswell
Drapes for *Le nozze di Figaro* by Ken Creasey
Property buyer for *Le nozze di Figaro* Sarah Alfandary-Joseph
Specialist rigging for *Le nozze di Figaro* by The Unusual Rigging Company
Specialist Lighting and effects by Howard Eaton Lighting Ltd
Stage Machinery by Peter Kemp Engineers
Champagne for *Arabella* by Moët et Chandon
Spectacles supplied by Grice Gwatkin, Uckfield
Pianos maintained and tuned by David Guy and Michael Gamble
Harpsichord maintained by Robert Goble & Son Ltd and tuned by Michael Gamble

Harpsichords hired from Mark Ransom for *Le nozze di Figaro* and from Michael Gamble
Pit Manager Emily Stubbs
Supertitles for *Jenůfa* by Peter Bloor, originally for the Royal Opera House, Covent Garden, edited for Glyndebourne by Sarah Plummer
Supertitles operated by Sarah Plummer, Gillian Brierley and Alexander Hayesmore
The John Player Special Marquee Pavillion is maintained by John M Carter Ltd

Glyndebourne wishes to thank

The Ford Motor Co Ltd and Endeavour Fleet & Leasing Operations for their help with transport vehicles
Marley Limited for their continued generous help with floor coverings
Cimex International Ltd for the provision of floor-cleaning equipment
L'Oreal for the provision of Elnett Hairspray
Lever Bros for the provision of Persil and Stergene for use in the wardrobe.
Taylor of London for the provision of pot pourri in the Organ Room

Front of House Staff

Box Office Staff:
Frances Edy
Evelyn Gray
Anita Kettle
Jenny KilBride
Jacky Lovill
Elisabeth Stern
Peter Walker

Information Office Assistants:
Kay Pollock
Pauline Burgiss
Doreen Court
Alison Tugman

General Office Assistant:
Caroline Giles

Assistant Chief Telephonist:
Margaret Marsh

Chief Ushers:
Keith Herbert
Ronald Bowman (Deputy)

Chief Fire Officer:
Vincent Richardson

Audience Car Park:
Harry Mitchell

Security:
Fred Riggs

Chief Driver:
Brian Middleton

Car Park Superintendent:
Derrick Clinkscales

Marquee Supervisor:
Rex Rogers

Assistant Gardener:
William Baldock

Maintenance and Cleaning:
Rosemary Phillips (Head Cleaner)
Nancy Parker
John Edwards
Trevor Emery
Ray Southwell

Head Plumber:
Lester Ripley

THE KOSTELNIČKA: A LIFE BEFORE AND AFTER

by John Tyrrell

The Kostelnička's appearance at the height of the festivities with which Števa celebrates his escape from being drafted into the army is one of the most dramatic moments in Janáček's opera *Jenůfa*. A forbidding figure, the Kostelnička steps onto the stage and with a simple motion of her hand stops the music and the dancing. Her message is that her foster-daughter Jenůfa – seen leading the dancing with the drunken Števa – will not have her permission to marry Števa until he has stopped drinking for a year. At this point the Kostelnička does not realize that Jenůfa is pregnant by Števa and her only hope of respectability is to marry him quickly. Even so, the Kostelnička's ban seems unduly punitive. The audience's view of the Kostelnička is bound to be the same as that of Grandmother Buryja, that her daughter-in-law is a '*přísná ženská*', a 'harsh woman'.

This, at any rate, is the interpretation that audiences from about 1908 until quite recently have formed of the Kostelnička. But the Kostelnička of the 1904 premiere of the opera was rather different. Once the dancing had stopped she sang a short aria explaining her actions. In it she declared that Števa and his behaviour reminded her of her own late husband, whose drunken gambling had reduced her to penury. The last thing she wanted was for her beloved foster-daughter Jenůfa to suffer as she did: Jenůfa may marry only a reformed Števa. The aria humanizes the Kostelnička. She comes across not as authoritarian, puritanical, even malevolent, but as energetic, caring and practical.

Janáček cut this aria when he revised the score for publi-cation in 1908, and with good reason. The aria holds up the action. Without it, the Kostelnička's brief and devastating appearance is a superb coup-de-théâtre. But its loss means that the character is even further removed from the Kostelnička in Gabriela Preissová's play. Even before this cut, the Kostelnička was the character who had changed most in Janáček's adaptation of the play. In order to reduce the text to manageable proportions he left out a number of small parts and incidents whose purpose was mainly to throw light on the character of the Kostelnička. Act 2 in the opera, for example, is confined to one claustrophobic room with just the four main characters, giving it maximum force and concentration. The play, on the other hand, includes in this act a visit to the Kostelnička by a woman worried by the philanderings of her husband at the local pub. The Kostelnička has remarkably open-minded advice to offer: see that he doesn't have too much money with him, so he won't be able to do much harm, and just wait it out – he'll soon tire of his barmaid. A scene omitted from Act 1 describes how the Kostelnička has recently been nursing a little girl dying of diphtheria.

From all this detail one can infer that the Kostelnička is a practical person, who serves in the village as agony aunt and medical practitioner. She is full of good works from which, despite her poverty, she makes no material profit. All this puts her ban on Jenůfa's marriage into a more sympathetic context. It also makes her fall all the more tragic and not the thoroughly deserved punishment for the holier-than-thou hypocrite that she is sometimes portrayed as.

121

In these and many other ways the play skilfully hints at a past history of the Kostelnička, a history that has been all but obliterated by Janáček's adaptation of the text. Forty years after the premiere of the play in 1890, and thus long after the world success of Janáček's opera based on it, the now elderly Preissová wrote a novel, bearing the same title as her play *Její pastorkyňa* – 'Her foster-daughter'. Many passages in the novel do little more than reprint the dialogue of the characters of the play. But, most interestingly, Preissová's novel also spells out in considerable detail events only hinted at in the play. The past history which shaped the Kostelnička's distinctive personality is presented as a chronicle taking up virtually the first half of the novel.

In the novel we learn her real name – Petrona Slomková. The novel starts with a description of the local castle, and then moves on to the Slomek cottage. It is suggested that Petrona's father, sometime mayor of the village, has noble connections. There is a portrait in the castle that the young Petrona, on a rare visit to the Countess, thinks looks very much like her father. Another significant incident occurs when the old Countess summons Slomek to her at the castle. She is near death, and beset by fears. All her expensive town doctors can suggest is for her to take the air at another of her estates – presumably beyond their responsibility. But Slomek, who has a reputation as a folk physician, talks to her simply and straightforwardly 'as a brother', explaining how she need have no fear, and she is comforted. She knows that he will accept no reward and instead she gives him a picture of their common ancestor and takes her leave of him with a kiss, 'as a sister'. Both die shortly after. Petrona, rather than her older married sister, inherits her father's sizable small-holding as well as his gifts as a folk physician, herbalist and counsellor.

The purpose of this long prehistory is to suggest that Petrona has special blood in her veins that sets her apart from the rest of the village (the play even specified that she talks in 'a more exalted tone' than the others). The novel also stresses her independence of spirit, her strong character, and the tough life ordained by her father's wish to bring her up as if she were the boy he wanted. Unlike her sister, Petrona remains unmarried. She is almost thirty when she shows some interest in a man, though after a brief flirtation, he abruptly goes off and marries Jenůfa, the daughter of an inn-keeper from a neighbouring village.

That man was Tomáš ('Tóma') Buryja, of the local mill family. His brother is the miller, and Tóma leads the life of an attractive, idle younger son. His marriage, however, is shortlived and his wife dies, leaving him with a six-week-old daughter, the little Jenůfa. In these circumstances Petrona cannot refuse his urgent and humble request to give Jenůfa

a mother, although she is well aware of his many shortcomings. At first Tóma appears to be a changed personality under the firm, sensible rule of his second wife. To build up his confidence, she has half her property made out in his name. This is a mistake. One day, seven weeks after the marriage, she sends Tóma off with a large sum of money to buy an adjacent piece of land. But he falls in with his old cronies and the money disappears in a wild gambling spree. From then on his path is only downwards. Within two years he has drunk and gambled his way through most of his wife's wealth, and dies in a shooting accident.

Petrona Buryjovka, as she has become, has been shaken by all this, but not deterred from her principles and she brings up her step-daughter Jenůfa in a model fashion. Now very poor, she is forced to make a living by her embroidery and by taking and selling groceries to the nearby town – in the original play she is first seen with a large basket strapped to her back. The priest of the local town (there is none in the tiny hamlet of Bystranka, where the novel is set), is so impressed by her exemplary behaviour that he asks her to serve as sacristan in the local chapel, dedicated to St Anthony. It is from this that Petrona Slomková derives her title of 'Kostelnička' (lady sacristan), by which she is generally known. She continues, as her father did, to give advice to those in trouble, to dispense herbal remedies and to use her nursing skills for those in need. And she looks ahead to the time when her beloved young foster-daughter might get married.

From an early stage it seems likely she will marry her

cousin Ladislav ('Laca') Klemeň. Tóma's older brother, the miller, had married a widow with a young son, Laca. Although older than the miller's own son, Števa, Laca has no claim to the mill, where he is apprenticed, and can hope only for a small inheritance from his father when he comes of age. Laca is sensible and hardworking. He is attracted to his pretty cousin Jenůfa, and recognizes the qualities of her step-mother. He is a frequent visitor at the Slomek cottage, helping the Kostelnička with some of the more demanding chores around the house and her much reduced plot. By the time that Laca is twenty-two and has to go off for military service (conscription at that time in the Austrian army was three years), there is an understanding between him and Jenůfa and the Kostelnička that on his return he will marry Jenůfa.

But things have changed when he comes back from the army. Jenůfa is now an attractive young woman of nineteen. During Laca's absence her head has been turned by Laca's younger half-brother Števa. Števa's father, the miller, has died of pneumonia, and Števa is now the owner of the family mill. He is a rich catch, and with his golden hair, a handsome one, though lazy and spoilt by his indulgent family. With Jenůfa now transferring her affections to Števa, Laca has even more reason to feel jealous and embittered. Jenůfa is embarrassed, but cannot help her feelings, and anyway is pregnant with Števa's child. All of them are waiting to see the outcome of the annual conscription formalities. If Števa, whose turn it now is to be called up, has to go off, then Laca can still hope that Jenůfa

will eventually change her mind. Jenůfa has of course more urgent reasons for hoping that Števa might be spared. This is the situation when the curtain opens.

At the end of the play and at the end of the opera, Jenůfa once again agrees to marry Laca, now sure of his love for her, a love that has survived the shaming revelations of the Kostelnička's confessions. For Jenůfa, her passive acceptance of his proposal, at the time virtually an arranged marriage, now turns to love. The wounds of her painful process of learning and growing have been healed. In her novel, Gabriela Preissová takes the story a little further. After Števa's escape from conscription, Laca goes off to work in the mill of a neighbouring village. He decides to take his young bride there, and leave behind them the scene of so much sadness. They settle down, Laca hires his own mill and starts a family. But what of the Kostelnička?

According to the novel, the jury sentences Petrona Buryjovka to two years in prison. The judges accept the defence's claim that the unhappy woman acted in a fit when her senses were confused. Everyone is struck by the fact that at no time does she try to deny her guilt. As the judge pronounces her sentence, she stays silent, her eyes constantly fixed to the ground, and she reacts audibly and with anguish only to the mention of her father, the long-time mayor of Bystranka. At the end of her prison sentence, Jenůfa and Laca take her with them to their new home. She recovers her spirits a little there, but when told that Jenůfa is expecting a child she turns pale and begins trembling. She does not live to see the birth of her new grandson.

*Keine Idylle, Eisenrad
Ziegelbau
Die Mühle bzw. die aus ihr
resultierenden Machtverhältnisse
bestimmen das Verhältnis der
Figuren*

Pages from Jenůfa *sketchbook by Tobias Hoheisel*

Burger auf einem Schemel i.d.
untergehenden Sonne vor der
Holzwand Kartoffelholz etc.

1. Akt

Böschung teil
weise begehbar
dahinter Steg

Spätnachmittag eine einsame Mühle im
Gebirge

mit Ochsenblut gestrichene Holzwand
Böschung mit gelblich-grünem Spätsommer-
gras, zum Mühlbach an der schwärz-
lichen Matsch. über dem Bach ein paar
Borettes darüber Jenůfa

Pages from Jenůfa *sketchbook by Tobias Hoheisel © 1988*

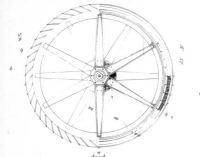

*Technical drawing and
costume design by
Tobias Hoheisel © 1988*

The conclusion of the Kostelnička's tale is of course the invention of the author, Gabriela Preissová. Although scrupulous in her description of village life in Moravian Slovakia, where novel, play and opera are set, her view of what punishment the Kostelnička could expect for her crime is somewhat different from the realities of the law. In this article, by Dr Richard Klos, who until his retirement was the leading Czech lawyer involved with the copyrights of Janáček's works, an attempt is made to establish what in real life might have happened to the Kostelnička. For his purpose Dr Klos confines his evidence to the play alone. The opera, he argues, simply takes over Preissová's information and does not attempt to change any aspect relevant to such a consideration. And the novel, written long after the play, he regards as a sentimental prettification, distorted by several anachronisms.

JT

THE KOSTELNIČKA'S SENTENCE: A LAWYER'S VIEW

by Richard Klos

The basis of the accusation is known: the accused (the Kostelnička), driven by complicated motives, has drowned a baby – the illegitimate child of her foster-daughter Jenůfa.

To clarify her action we must – as in a detective story – answer five questions: who?, where?, when?, what? and how? We know the answer to the first question. Even without further personal details we know that the offender was a simple villager and was thus subject to the common criminal law. It is also enough for us to localize the action to southern Moravia, since up to 1918 it belonged to the Austro-Hungarian monarchy and was thus subject to

Austrian criminal law. We can equally answer the questions 'what crime?' (the deliberate murder of a child) and 'how?' (by drowning).

It is more difficult to answer the question 'when?'. This would resolve what criminal law was in force at the time, according to which the crime and punishment would be determined. The evidence, which we will examine, does not provide an unequivocal answer and we will have to deduce an answer by assessing the merits of various factors. The question is important because in the nineteenth century Austrian criminal law changed in 1803 and in 1852, apart from smaller updatings.

Both the libretto and the play are hampered by certain shared anachronisms, one could say historical errors. The most important and striking of these, in comparison with other indications of the time of the action, is the existence of the *rychtař* (mayor). The office of *rychtař* was abolished by the local constitution of 17 March 1849 (together with the post of *purkmistr* – burgomaster – of which there is also talk). The mayor says of himself: 'Mine is the first office'. From 1850 his successor, the parish representative or *starosta*, could not say this and would not be allowed to. Sometimes there is talk of 'lords' (as if the patrimonial administration and method of justice abolished in 1848 still existed), but at the end of the libretto and the play the mayor talks about '*soud*' (judgement, evidently by the state). The question then arises whether the action ought not to take place before 1848-9. When however we take into account the fact that after 1874 Gabriela Preissová spent more than ten years in Hodonín and probably got to know then the realities of village life in the surrounding countryside, it would seem that the nomenclature for the post of mayor and other statements were simply survivals of long-established terminology. Similarly today in many places in the Czech countryside they like to call the chairman of the National Council '*starosta*', although that post disappeared in 1945. In neither the play nor the libretto is there any mention of *robota* (forced labour) abolished in 1848, or even of the Austro-Prussian war of 1866. These historical realities were thus already a thing of the past. We do not need to place the crime before the year 1848, simply because of the mayor's title, especially as there are important pointers to a later period. These, moreover, are easy to date.

Decisive circumstances for the plot of the play and the libretto include Laca's 3-year military service and the fact that Števa avoided conscription. A three-year period of military service was brought into the Austro-Hungarian monarchy by the defence law of 1868 and it was still in force up to the time of the premiere of the play (before 1868 military service lasted eight years). The system of conscription corresponding to references in the play and the libretto came into force at the same time. Laca could not then have returned from three years' military service before 1868, and Števa would have undergone conscription at the earliest in 1868. Thus the time of the action as far as its earliest date is concerned can be limited quite precisely. It is clear that much more important facts than merely the title of the mayor would point to the 1870s rather than to before 1848. We have thus arrived at a period close to Preissová's stay in Hodonín. Janáček's cuts in making the libretto do not affect the indications for this period; it seems that he did not wish to change the time of the action.

The question 'when?' is therefore sufficiently clarified: after 1868 (defence law) and before 1890 (premiere of the

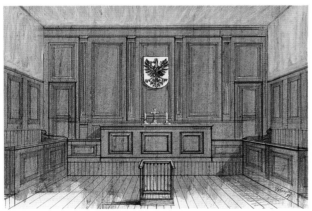

Sketch by Vobejda of a 19th century Moravian courthouse

play). For the Kostelnička's trial this would mean using the Austrian criminal law of 1852 (which was still in force long into the twentieth century) to determine her punishment. One thing we cannot ascertain is whether a jury would have taken part in the decision. After their temporary abolition in 1852, juries were reinstated by the criminal law of 1873 and there is nothing in the play to indicate whether the action took place before or after 1873. There was no difference in the decision-making: the same criminal law was used in each case. It was said, however, that trials by jury were sometimes rather more lenient.

A decision about the punishment is predetermined by how you define the deed and this is unmistakable in the play and the libretto: it is the deliberate taking of human life, in other words, murder according to paragraph 134 of the above-mentioned criminal code, and moreover 'simple' murder (ie. not merely attempted murder, or 'qualified' murder for instance involving conspiracy, robbery etc). Simple murder was punished according to paragraph 136

of the code only by death. We must decide whether the circumstances of the case would have allowed a more lenient conclusion.

Above all the Kostelnička acted while in a difficult and prolonged state of emotion. From the texts of both play and libretto it is however impossible anywhere to conclude that she could be considered, even temporarily, as mentally ill, and thus irresponsible and unpunishable. During her crime and afterwards she behaved logically and cleverly, and managed for quite a long time to conceal the action; she even gave herself up calmly to punishment.

Her emotional state was created by fears for the reputation and future of Jenůfa (this aspect is emphasized in the opera by the choice of texts that Janáček made), by fears for her own prestige (which Janáček also of course did not suppress), and finally by sympathy for the child, which because of his illegitimacy could expect discrimination in the village. At this time these were real fears and palpable prejudices, especially in view of the difficult social standing of the Kostelnička and Jenůfa.

The Kostelnička's emotional state would therefore surely have been recognized as a mitigating factor and the judge would undoubtedly have accepted as a further extenuating circumstance the Kostelnička's oppressive poverty. The previous good reputation of the offender and her irreproachable behaviour would also be taken into account. From her actions at the end of the opera one could presume that she would fully admit her crime at the trial and this would count as a further mitigating factor.

One could summarize perhaps in this way: there is clear evidence of the crime of simple murder, and a number of mitigating factors. The law however was harsh (and so it remained for a long time after, up to the Czechoslovak revision in 1934) and gave no possibility to the judge other than a sentence of death.

The only alternative was a moderation of the sentence by a grant of clemency from the Austrian emperor, if the judges (and many further factors) recommended it. Even then it would have been difficult to arrive at a punishment less than some ten to fifteen years' hard labour (and the law then did not recognize today's conditional release for good behaviour).

At the end of the opera the relationship of Jenůfa and Laca does not break down, the main culprit Števa is punished (if only a little), the Kostelnička goes with resignation to her trial. Nevertheless it seems that the idea of an absolute punishment threatening the Kostelnička, reinforced by the due process of law, perceptibly intensifies the tragedy of Janáček's *Jenůfa* beyond our normal experience of it in the opera house.

A note by John Tyrrell on the score used in these performances can be found on page 101

127

Gluck

Orpheus, Euridice and Hermes;
marble, 5th century BC

GLUCK
THE REFORMER

by Jane Glover

Glancing across the centuries at the behaviour of the oper-atic animal, it does appear that there is an element in it of the wild beast. Opera was the invention of a committee, and an academic one at that, and devised on the basis of several principles, if not rules. But the monster that the committee created soon developed a mind, and indeed passions, of its own, energies that could really only be tamed by the most expert of masters. And thus opera has continued since its birth. It has repeatedly broken away from its fundamental principles, and required disciplinary attention. But on every occasion the action taken, however harsh it may have seemed, has performed the function of rescuing opera from self-destruction, and so ensured its continued journey through musical and theatrical history.

Opera evolved at the end of the sixteenth century, at the hands of a group of Florentine intellectuals known as the Camerata. They included scientists and philosophers as well as poets and musicians, and they met regularly, rather in the manner of a Bloomsbury group, to discuss philos-ophy, literature and the arts. Their interest in the Greek dramas of classical antiquity, which they believed to have been largely sung rather than spoken, led them to try and rediscover a means of combining music, drama, dance and spectacular staging into an integrated and balanced theatrical entertainment. And so they created *dramma in musica*, an art-form where the aggregate exceeded the sum of its component parts. For its earliest experiments, the Camerata significantly chose to tell the Orpheus legend, which lent itself so naturally to a musical narration; and indeed it was this same story which was the basis of the first operatic masterpiece, Monteverdi's *Orfeo* of 1607 (astonish-ingly, only a decade after the first fumbling and somewhat self-conscious essays on the part of the Camerata).

Gradually opera spread through Italy, first via the courtly circuit, and then, especially in Venice, into the public theatres. Composers, librettists and designers threw them-selves with tremendous vigour into what became a fast industry of opera, and by the mid-seventeenth century the product was a highly sophisticated and balanced entertain-ment of enormous popular appeal. But soon the wild beast began to strain at its leash. In the course of the next cen-tury, the various individual components of opera were severally emphasised and overdeveloped, at the expense of the others, thus distorting the basic veracity of the operatic equation. First it was the singers who (egged on, certainly, by their audiences) wrought the destruction: they

Liberatio Eurydicis.

128

demanded ever greater opportunities to show off their vocal gifts and expertise. Arias became longer, more stylised in structure, and altogether more flamboyant in display; but their general relationship to the dramatic situation became more remote, with the result that, already, music and drama began to part company. Understandably, librettists grew bitter and cynical about their reduced role in the creating of a theatrical event (as early as 1665 one had even complained in print about '*gli humori stavaganti dei Signori Musici recitanti*'), but they had no option but to resign themselves to their subservience. So they constructed their texts to formulae, both of dramatic plot (the required pairings of princely lovers, elements of disguise, intrigue and so on) and of poetic gesture. And then the visual element began to dominate, especially in France. Such were the advances in stage machinery and design that an opera production was often evaluated on the quality and indeed quantity of its different scene changes, and not on its musical or dramatic worth. Taken on their own terms, of course, these developments were extremely exciting, as were the developments in singers' techniques and their abilities therefore to achieve phenomenal vocal feats. But in the context of music-drama, and simple theatrical truth, they were only imbalancing.

By the eighteenth century the conventions were even more defined and restricting. The main dramatic argument was carried in dialogue, set as *recitativo secco*. This was regularly interrupted by reflective or commentary arias on single poetic images, and the protracted *da capo* structure of these gave singers considerable scope for embellishment and extemporisation. The plots of these serious operas (*opera seria*) generally concerned the great heroes of antiquity, whose activities, whether political, military or domestic, were imbued with an edifying moral tone. After the required amount of suffering and anguish the operas generally ended happily: the old seventeenth-century custom of the *lieto fine* persisted into the eighteenth century (opera was after all show business, and it was important to send the audience out of the theatre in a good mood). Yet for all the rigidity of the conventions, the operas of the early eighteenth century were by no means without merit. The distinguished court poet Pietro Metastasio was a master of the formula: his 27 librettos are highly skilful works which not only satisfied the requirements of this strange entertainment, but did so with considerable poetic grace and elegance. They were so successful that they were set to music time and again (his *Artaserse* was probably the most popular, and even boasts a setting in an English translation, by Thomas Arne in 1762). Gluck was to set several Meta-

Orpheus in the underworld: from a Greek amphora

stasio texts, and so, of course, was Mozart, with *La clemenza di Tito*. And in the first half of the eighteenth century, it was Handel who most conspicuously succeeded in transcending the restrictions of the *opera seria* convention, and produced theatrical music of genuine distinction.

But despite these achievements and the continuing success of the operatic medium in this artificial form, the fact remains that the opera ideal was now very far from its original conception. Clearly something fairly drastic would have to be done to tug the wayward creature back on to its original course; and it would be a gesture of consummate bravery on the part of whoever did so, in the face of such popularity. Christoph Willibald Gluck was born in 1714, and so grew up in the heyday of *opera seria*, even contributing to its continuation in the early part of his career. When, in *Orfeo ed Euridice* in his 48th year, he performed the essential task of restoring opera to its original criteria, it was a seriously considered act based on decades of experience and growing discontent.

In many ways Gluck seems a most unlikely candidate for this historic role. Unlike most of his colleagues in court in Vienna, he was not born into a family of musicians. He was the son of a forester and huntsman, and it was generally assumed that he too would pursue an outdoor career. But a love of music and a determination to explore it fully caused Gluck to run away from home at the age of only thirteen (an early indication, surely, of courageous resolve) and to settle in Prague. As he grew up there, he heard the Italian operas of Vivaldi and Albinoni, and so acquired the first level of knowledge upon which his operatic career would be based. After a short spell in Vienna in his early 20s, he was engaged as a 'cellist by the Italian nobleman Antonio Maria Prince Melzi, for his orchestra in Milan. And so Gluck spent several years in the country that was still the heart of the opera world. In 1741, when he was 27, he had his first operatic chance: he was asked to set the ubiquitous *Artaserse* text by Metastasio, for the Teatro Regio Ducal in Milan. It was a brilliant success, and led to a steady stream of commissions for similar operas in cities throughout Italy. In 1745 he was invited to London, where he produced two operas (largely constructed in haste of material taken from existing works) for the Theatre Royal in the Haymarket, and provoked the celebrated if unfair comment from the 60-year-old *éminence grise*, Handel, that "Gluck knows no more of counterpoint than my cook". He continued to travel throughout Europe between 1746 and 1752, writing successful operas wherever he went (including a setting of Metastasio's *La clemenza di Tito* for Naples in 1752).

Eventually he entered the service of the Prince of Saxe-Hildburghausen in Vienna, at the end of 1752. Thus he became Konzertmeister to an august and energetic patron of the arts, and acquired a sure foothold on the musical ladder in the city which, under the Empress Maria Theresa, was fast becoming the cultural capital of Europe.

Like many musicians, including Haydn and Mozart, who followed Gluck in Vienna in the latter part of the eighteenth century, Gluck benefited enormously from the richness of artistic and literary exchange in the city. Through giving concerts for his patron at the magnificent Palais Rofrano, he gradually met such distinguished personalities as Count Durazzo and Count Kaunitz (both avid artistic thinkers and promoters) and also the great Metastasio himself. Durazzo in particular was fascinated by current operatic trends in France, now concentrating on *opéra comique* with its lighter plots, and greater emphasis on dancers and the chorus; and it was he who engaged Gluck to adapt specific French works to Viennese taste. Thus Gluck acquired considerably wider operatic experience,

Orpheus and the animals by J Bouttats, late 17th century

Orpheus by J Delville, late 19th century

Bridgeman Art Library/Giraudon/Gillion-Crouvet, Brussels

both in the traditional *opera seria* mould (for example his setting of Metastasio's *Le cinesi* in 1754) and of a comic nature (as in his *La fausse esclave* of 1758 at the Burgtheater).

But it was Durazzo's passionate desire to mould the greatest characteristics of Italian and French opera into a new and improved form that led him eventually to bring together the three crucial personalities who would effect the task: a poet, a musician and a choreographer. He introduced Gluck first to the choreographer Gaspero Angiolini, and then to the poet Raniero Calzabigi, an Italian who had worked in France. These three men found that, while they certainly shared enormous admiration for Metastasio and his achievements (Calzabigi had indeed produced a complete edition of his works in Paris in 1755), they were all fundamentally disturbed by the state of opera as they now found it, by the formalism of its plots, the restrictive nature of its musical structures, and by the vanity of its executors whose chief requirement of a role was that it should demonstrate their supreme virtuosity. Further, this formidable triumvirate of Gluck, Calzabigi and Angiolini was thoroughly aware of the proto-Romantic shift that was rippling through European culture and philosophy: of the rising emotion and enthusiasm that was to mark a general retreat from the elegance of the Enlightenment, and (among so many other movements) a return to naturalism and truth. And so, after their first collaboration in 1761, the hugely successful ballet *Don Juan* for the Burgtheater, they finally took the noble and courageous step of putting theory into practice in 1762, when they produced *Orfeo ed Euridice*.

Given that it was the first attempt of Gluck and Calzabigi to restore opera to its true function, of simply telling a dramatic story in music (*dramma in musica*), the achievements of *Orfeo ed Euridice* are astonishing. First, they realligned the structure of the opera's participants. They limited the protagonists to the absolute minimum of three, but balanced these with the return of a contributing chorus and a *corps de ballet* (as in French opera). Secondly, they completely abandoned the *recitativo secco/da capo* aria convention, replacing it with a text which unfolds at a naturalistic pace, whether a slow, tragic one (as in the opening of Act 1, with Orfeo's simple strophic aria punctuated by accompanied recitatives), or a fast one (as in the conversation which develops into veritable domestic argument between Orfeo and Euridice at the beginning of Act 3). And, despite the fact that the role of Orfeo was written for a specific virtuoso singer, the celebrated castrato Gaetano Guadagni, there was simply no occasion allowed for vocal exhibitionism to interrupt the dramatic flow. In general,

131

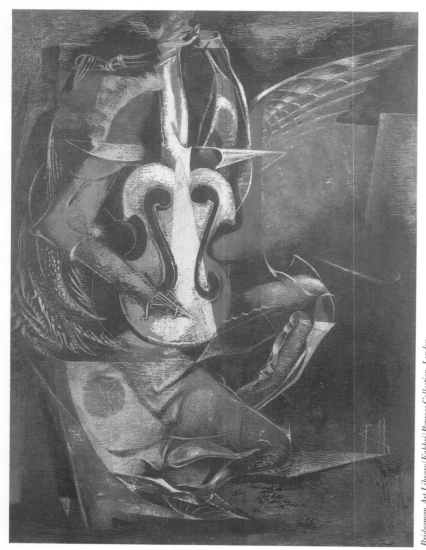

'Black music' by Roland Penrose

Gluck constructed his melodies of the utmost simplicity: '*Che farò senza Euridice*' is the most celebrated example of this lyrical refinement; and, significantly, where there is an occasion for the easing of dramatic tension, at Orfeo's passing from the realms of Hades into the Elysian fields, the sense of release and wonder is expressed by Orfeo in the most remarkable number in the opera, '*Che puro ciel*', with its extreme purity supported by the most alluring instrumental textures. Indeed, Gluck's orchestration throughout the opera is both imaginative and yet unobtrusive, recalling the best moments of his French predecessors Lully and Rameau, and, though he cannot have known it, the achievements of that first genius of the Orpheus legend in opera, Monteverdi.

Orfeo ed Euridice is remarkable, then, for the boldness of its rejection of convention. But the festive nature of the first performance of the opera (it was given to celebrate the Emperor's name-day on 5 October, 1762) did mean that Gluck and Calzabigi could not go quite as far as they clearly wished in the telling of a tragic tale. For this reason the overture is brisk and celebratory, and the true, appalling end to the legend of Orpheus (where he is torn to death by a band of Mænads) had to be abandoned in favour of a more conventional *lieto fine*. (All Gluck's predecessors in Orpheus operas, it should be added, had similarly bypassed the original ending.) But in their next collaboration, *Alceste* of 1768, Gluck and Calzabigi were able to carry out their reforms to a much greater degree; and Gluck then took the opportunity, in his celebrated Preface to the publication of the opera, to explain the measures they had taken. In a prose style as elegantly direct as that of his music, Gluck presented his arguments with gentle precision. His mission, he stated, was to divest opera of "all those abuses, introduced into it either by the mistaken vanity of singers or by too great complaisance of composers, which have so long disfigured Italian opera and made of the most splendid and most beautiful of spectacles the most ridiculous and wearisome". He continued: "I have striven to restrict music to its true office of serving poetry by means of expression and by following the situations of the story, without interrupting the action or stifling it with a useless superfluity of ornaments; and I believed that it should do this in the same way as telling colours affect a correct and well-ordered drawing, by a well-assorted contrast of light and shade, which serves to animate the figures without altering their contours." He generously acknowledged the achievements of Calzabigi for having provided "heartfelt language, strong passions, interesting situations and an endlessly varied spectacle". And he concluded with his admirable credo, that "simplicity, truth and naturalness are the great principles of beauty in all artistic manifestations".

A MIDSUMMER NIGHT'S DREAM ANTHOLOGY

compiled by Donald Mitchell and Philip Reed

The Composer's *Dream*

Britten's *A Midsummer Night's Dream*, Op. 64, in three acts, with a libretto adapted from Shakespeare by the composer and Peter Pears, was first performed by the English Opera Group at the Jubilee Hall, during the 13th Aldeburgh Festival, on 11 June 1960. The opera was produced by John Cranko, designed by John Piper, and conducted by Britten. The work was dedicated to Stephen Reiss. A week before the premiere, Britten contributed the following article to *The Observer* (5 June) – one of the very few occasions on which Britten wrote about one of his works in the press:

Last August it was decided that for this year's Aldeburgh Festival I should write a full-length opera for the opening of the reconstructed Jubilee Hall.

As this was a comparatively sudden decision there was no time to get a libretto written, so we took one that was ready to hand. I get a lot of letters from young people asking me how they should use their talents, and I always reply that they should try to fit them into their surroundings. This is what has happened with my new opera. It is an example of how local conditions can determine what you do.

I have always loved *A Midsummer Night's Dream*.

As I get older, I find that I increasingly prefer the work either of the very young or of the very old. I always feel *A Midsummer Night's Dream* to be by a very young man, whatever Shakespeare's actual age when he wrote it. Operatically, it is especially exciting because there are three quite separate groups – the lovers, the rustics, and the fairies – which nevertheless interact. Thus in writing the opera I have used a different kind of texture and orchestral 'colour' for each section. For instance, the fairies are accompanied by harps and percussion; though obviously with a tiny orchestra they can't be kept absolutely separate.

In writing opera, I have always found it very dangerous to start writing the music until the words are more or less fixed. One talks to a possible librettist, and decide together the shape of the subject and its treatment. In my case, when I worked with E M Forster or William Plomer, for instance, we blocked the opera out in the way that an artist might block out a picture. With *A Midsummer Night's Dream*, the first task was to get it into a manageable shape, which basically entailed simplifying and cutting an extremely complex story – one can only hope that one hasn't lost too much, but since the sung word takes so much longer than the spoken word, to have done the complete *A Midsummer Night's Dream* would have produced an opera as long as the *Ring*.

Peter Pears (who sings Flute, the bellows-mender) and I had endless trouble with the references and the proportions of the play. We stuck faithfully to Shakespeare's words, actually adding only one line: 'Compelling thee to marry with Demetrius'. We worked from many texts, but principally from facsimiles of the First Folio and the First Quarto.

I do not feel in the least guilty at having cut the play in half. The original Shakespeare will survive. Nor did I find it daunting to be tackling a masterpiece which already has a strong verbal music of its own. Its music and the music I have written for it are at two quite different levels. I haven't tried to put across any particular idea of the play that I could equally well express in words, but although one doesn't intend to make any special interpretation, one cannot avoid it.

The opera is more relaxed than *The Turn of the Screw*; it has far more scenes, and is much less uniform. In form, it is more like *Peter Grimes*. I have felt it to be a more difficult task to write than these, partly because the work in hand is always the hardest, partly because of the tremendous challenge of those Shakespearean words. Working at it, one was very conscious that one must not let through a single ill-considered phrase because it would be matched to such great poetry.

I actually started work on the opera in October, and finished it on, I think, Good Friday – seven months for everything, including the score. This is not up to the speed of Mozart or Verdi, but these days, when the line of musical language is broken, it is much rarer. It is the fastest of any big opera I have written, though I wrote *Let's Make an Opera* in a fortnight.

Writing an opera is very different from writing individual songs: opera, of course, includes songs, but has many other musical forms and a whole dramatic shape as well. In my experience, the shape comes first. With *A Midsummer Night's Dream*, as with other operas, I first had a general musical conception of the whole work in my mind. I conceived the work without any one note being defined. I could have described the music, but not played a note.

It was a particularly bad winter for me, writing it. Normally I work perfectly regular hours, in the morning and again between four and eight in the evening. Around Aldeburgh, the weather seems always to be better in the morning; it clouds over about midday and I don't work then. I cannot work at night. In Suffolk the air is strong, and by nightfall I want to do nothing but sleep. This

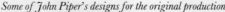
Some of John Piper's designs for the original production

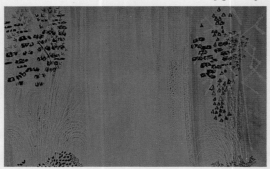

winter I became quite ill, but had to go on working. A lot of the third act was written when I was not at all well with 'flu. I didn't enjoy it. But I find that one's inclination, whether one wants to work or not, does not in the least affect the quality of the work done. Very often it is precisely after one has had what one feels to have been a wonderful morning, that one needs to watch out – perhaps one's critical faculties may have been asleep.

I haven't tried to give the opera an Elizabethan flavour. It is no more Elizabethan than Shakespeare's play was Athenian. Perhaps one or two points may seem strange. The fairies, for instance, are very different from the innocent nothings that often appear in productions of Shakespeare. I have always been struck by a kind of sharpness in Shakespeare's fairies; besides, they have some odd poetry to speak – the part about 'you spotted snakes with double tongue' for instance. The fairies are, after all, the guards to Tytania: so they have, in places, martial music. Like the actual world, incidentally, the spirit world contains bad as well as good.

Puck is quite a different character from anyone else in the play. He seems to me to be absolutely amoral and yet innocent. In this production he is being played by the 15-year-old son of Leonide Massine: he doesn't sing, but only speaks and tumbles about. I got the idea of doing Puck like this in Stockholm, where I saw some Swedish child acrobats with extraordinary agility and powers of mimicry, and suddenly realized we could do Puck that way.

The opera, since it was written for a hall which holds only 316 people, is small-scale. The forces one uses must necessarily be small, which has great advantages: one can work in a more detailed way with them and get a greater degree of discipline. The singers do not have to sing with such uniform volume, so that the voice can be used throughout its full range of colour. Besides, on a small scale, we can choose singers who either can act or who are prepared to learn to do so. Some opera-goers seem to prefer singers who cannot act: there is a curious inverted snobbery current in this country which even prefers operatic

Carl Toms' costume design for Oberon

acting to be as bad as possible. they do not want opera to be serious at all. They like singers who merely come down to the footlights and yell.

For my part, I want singers who can act. Mozart, Gluck and Verdi wanted the same thing. There is one singer in this production who has never been on a stage before in his life; but his strong concert personality fits naturally on to the operatic stage and his acting is developing very well. How many singers know how to move? I think it's essential for every potential opera singer to have a course of movement in an opera school. I must say one hoped, after the war, that audiences would revolt at seeing opera performed with bad acting, bad scenery and in a foreign language.

We are taking *A Midsummer Night's Dream* to Holland immediately after the Aldeburgh Festival. If it is any good it will get many different interpretations in many different places and all with translations. I have even heard *Peter Grimes* in Serbo-Croat. But the new opera was really written as part of the Aldeburgh Festival, for the reopening of the Jubilee Hall. Ultimately, it is to me the local things that matter most.

Benjamin Britten

Documents

Pears first prepared for Britten a handwritten synopsis of the action of the play, which included calculations of the number of lines in each scene, and a list of characters. This was the very start of the project.

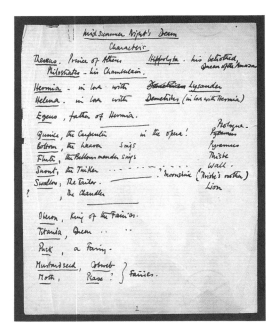

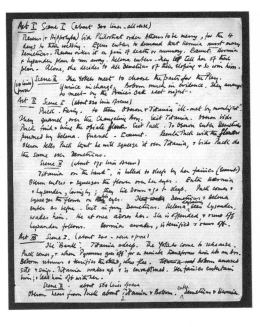

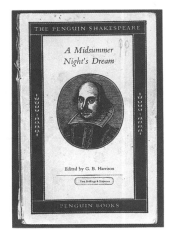

Britten and Pears each had a working copy of the Penguin edition of the play. We reproduce Pears's copy.

From Britten's copy, we reproduce the half-title on which he indicated where, in Shakespeare's text, Act 1 of the opera was to begin.

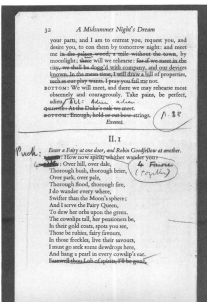

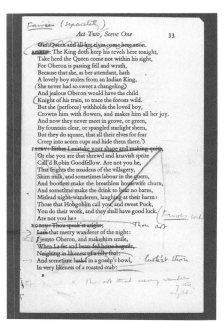

Pages 32 and 33, marked by Britten.

A page from Britten's typed libretto. His marks indicate his musical ideas for this passage, i.e. the promotion of Hermia's 'I swear to thee' to the status of a refrain. It is also here that Pears and Britten added one line of their own invention: 'Compelling thee to marry with Demetrius'.

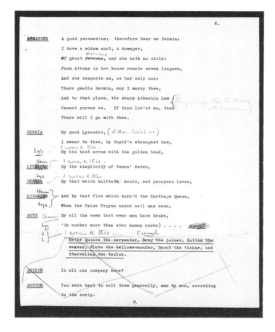

Britten's composition sketch: the opening of Act 1.

The opening of Act 2, with the famous sequence of 'Sleep' chords.

The close of Act 2, where the Fairies sing their lullaby, 'and all shall be well', over a rotation of the 'Sleep' chords.

Design
Some of the designs by John Piper and Carl Toms for the original production are shown on pages 134 and 135.

Photographs by Guy Gravett of the first production at Glyndebourne, 1981

The First Production

Act 1, the entrance of the Fairies

Particam

Act 3, the Rustics offering their
play to the Quality: Quince
(Norman Lumsden),
Bottom (Owen Brannigan),
Flute (Peter Pears),
Snout (Edward Byles),
Starveling (Joseph Ward) and
Snug (David Kelly)

Particam

Act 2, Tytania (Jennifer Vyvyan)
with Bottom in the Wood

Particam

Oberon
(Alfred
Deller) and
Tytania

Particam

Pears, Cranko and Britten, outside the Jubilee Hall, which is under reconstruction in preparation for the opera's premiere.

Leonide Massine II rehearsing Puck, a role allotted by Britten to a 'boy acrobat'

Keystone Press

The composer takes a bow after the first performance

Particam

The 'Sleep' Chords in Act 2

The world of sleep and dreams has a fundamental role to play in Shakespeare's comedy and Britten's opera. It is a world embodied in the four magical chords which open Act 2 and which Eric Roseberry showed to have an interesting history.

We know from the composer's own account [which we reproduce above] that work on *A Midsummer Night's Dream* was by no means always easy going. Therefore when I accidentally stumbled (aurally, be it noted) upon the remarkable fact that the four chords used in Act 2 of *The Dream* were almost identical with those used in the setting of Keats's sonnet '*To Sleep*' in the *Serenade* I fully expected to learn that the composer had consciously borrowed from the earlier work, reversing the order of the first two chords (adding a B to the D major chord) and magically re-spacing and re-scoring them. As the poetic element in each piece is concerned with the properties of sleep (inducing a healing forgetfulness on the one hand, a fantastic change of identities on the other) the conscious re-working of those earlier chords of the *Serenade* would have seemed by no means inapt.

But this proved not to be the case. The composer's reply to my letter drawing attention to the striking relationship offered material for much more subtle comment. He expressed amazement at the similarity of the chords – separated by seventeen years – which, he assured me, was purely subconscious. But what he found interesting was that whereas in the opera he had found it necessary consciously to use all the twelve semitones to create a four chord 'theme' (dramatically to make each chord sound a surprise, structurally as a basis for many variations), in the *Serenade* he had unconsciously arrived at the same chord series by a more instinctive technical process, i.e. "as a kind of harmonic overtone to the 'cello phrase'". Thus, as the music example below illustrates, Britten's own recent cautious approach to serialism is a development by no means unanticipated in the language of his earlier music, when he was quite unconcerned with the conscious application of this technique. Although it seems most unlikely that Britten will ever become wholly committed to serial organisation, the parallel with Schoenberg, who discovered twelve-note composition through creative practice, is evident.

Technical considerations apart, the close harmonic identity of the two passages discloses a remarkably precise and consistent musical response to the same poetic idea. And one is left marvelling at the quality of sheer inspiration, defying analytical comment.

Eric Roseberry
© *from* Tempo, *Autumn/Winter, 1963*

Wilfrid Mellers describes the two statements of the chords which frame the second act of the opera:

Act 2 deals with the effects of the spell on mortals and immortals, and Britten devises for it another exquisitely precise musical image. Four concordant but unrelated chords embrace every note of the chromatic scale and so, like the original forest murmurs, may be said to embrace a cosmos – that of the psyche in sleep. Each chord is allotted to a different instrumental group: D flat major to muted strings; D major with added sixth to muted brass; E flat major first inversion to woodwind; and a C major third to harps and 'magic' instruments. That the mind is multi-faceted is suggested by the way Britten opens the act, with four variations on these chords, incorporating barely perceptible hints of the lovers' motifs, of Oberon's seconds, and even of the Mechanicals' 'Rurall Musicke'. Perhaps it is not fortuitous that the bucolics first break the spell, clumping in for their rehearsal.

The chords return at the end of the act, as sleep overcomes the disorientated lovers, whose dreams will finally heal them:

> Puck's 'false' voice confuses the would-be aggressive young men so that, worn out by their wanderings in the wood, they again droop into sleep, to a recurrence of the spellbinding chord sequence. This time each chord is long sustained, supporting themes derived from the motif. Lysander has the fourth and third over the D flat major triad; Demetrius has it over the D major with added sixth; Helena has it, more simply, over the E flat first inversion. Puck momentarily takes over in bitonality between E flat and his habitual F sharp-D-A complex; while the fourth chord, the high C major third, is reserved for Hermia, emotionally most intense of the human characters. She has the most lyrically sustained version of the latent theme thus far. The act ends with the fairies singing a therapeutic lullaby over the sleepers, the chord sequence being reiterated several times both forwards and backwards, while the vocal incantation swings gently in parallel thirds. The static spell is thus imbued with some harmonic momentum; its remedial function is now operative.

> *Wilfrid Mellers*
> *from* The Britten Companion, *Faber 1984*

For the restoration of human relationships and the order of the universe Britten uses the basic resources of music in their totality:

> A feature of Britten's operatic *oeuvre* across the years was the expansion of his musical language and in particular the incorporation of twelve-note compilations into his armoury of expressive means. As his list of theatrical works inexorably lengthened, so was the methodical exploitation and organisation of all twelve pitches of the chromatic scale raised in profile. To both *Owen Wingrave* (1971) and *Death in Venice* (1973), for example, twelve-note 'propositions' (as John Evans, who has done important analytical work in this field, defines them) are fundamental to the compositional techniques – and to the dramatic character – of each opera. It cannot be repeated too often that Britten's twelve-note ideas are never, in the context of his operas, 'theoretical'

in practice but always have a specific dramatic association.

> A perfect example of this is to be found at the beginning of Act 2 of *A Midsummer Night's Dream*. The magical progression of four chords which opens the act unfolds all twelve pitches without repetition and represents, in its totality, the world of sleep and dreams. It is a world within which all the characters in the opera, for the duration of the act, have their being, the context in which we observe their trials and tribulations, their fortunes and their follies. Sleep closes the act, as it began it: but this time the rotation of the chords underpins the sublime lullaby of the Fairies, the promise that

> > Jack shall have Jill,
> > Naught shall go ill,
> > The man shall have his mare again,
> > And all shall be well.

> Here, surely, the totality of the musical materials has taken on an additional significance and represents not only the healing power of Sleep but also in some sense a restoration and reaffirmation of the *natural order of the universe*: at the end of Act 2 everyone and everything (*and all twelve pitches*) are in place, and the lovers can wake in Act 3 to the happiness which has hitherto eluded them in the labyrinth of the magic infested wood.

> *Donald Mitchell*
> *from the* Maggio Musicale Fiorentino Programme Book, 1988

Beaumarchais

Mozart

Hulton Picture Company

FIGARO – A PERFECT MARRIAGE

by David Cairns

Michael Kelly, the Irish tenor who played Basilio and Curzio in the first production of *Le nozze di Figaro*, has left a vivid picture of one of the rehearsals for the opera. It is a much quoted account but, for the Mozart lover, it will bear repetition.

Mozart was on the stage with his crimson pelisse and gold-laced cocked hat, giving the time of the music to the orchestra. Figaro's song '*non più andrai, farfallone amoroso*' Benucci gave with the greatest animation and power of voice. I was standing close to Mozart, who, *sotto voce*, was repeating "Bravo! Bravo! Benucci"; and when Benucci came to the fine passage '*Cherubino, alla vittoria, alla gloria militar*', which he gave out with Stentorian lungs, the effect was electricity itself; for the whole of the performers on the stage and those in the orchestra, as if actuated by one feeling of delight, vociferated "Bravo! Bravo! Maestro. Viva, viva, grande Mozart". The little man acknowledged, by repeated obeisances, the distinguished mark of enthusiastic applause bestowed on him.

If it is true that the singers to begin with were hostile to the work (as Mozart's early biographer Niemetschek claimed), this may well have been the moment when they came round to it. That would help to explain why Michael Kelly recalled the incident so clearly: it was a moment of shared electricity, when the genius of Mozart's music first dawned on them.

We may wonder why they could not have seen it at once. What could be more obviously inspired, more captivating, more natural than the musical language of *Figaro*? I

Angus McBean

"LE NOZZE DI FIGARO"

Count Almaviva	JOHN BROWNLEE (Australian)
The Countess	ELEANOR STEBER (American)
Susanna *(her maid)*	TATIANA MENOTTI (Italian)
Figaro	ITALO TAJO (Italian)
Cherubino *(a page)*	GIULIETTA SIMIONATO (Italian)
Bartolo *(a doctor)*	OWEN BRANNIGAN (British)
Marcellina *(his former housekeeper)*	CATHERINE LAWSON (British)
Basilio *(a music teacher)*	BRUCE FLEGG (British)
Antonio *(the count's gardener)*	ERNEST FRANK (British)
Barbarina *(his daughter and cousin to Susanna)*	BARBARA TRENT (British)
Don Curzio *(a lawyer)*	GWENT LEWIS (British)

THE GLYNDEBOURNE FESTIVAL CHORUS

THE SCOTTISH ORCHESTRA
Leader : JEAN RENNIE

Dance in Act III arranged by ERNEST BERK

remember so well my first delighted encounter with it, when Glyndebourne performed the work at the King's Theatre, Edinburgh in 1947. Right from the opening number I knew I had found something that would be a treasure all my life.

For the musicians of 1786, however, it was quite another experience. We think of Mozart's music as representing the typical, quintessential sound of the late 18th century, because he has eclipsed nearly all his contemporaries except Haydn. But to the Viennese of his time *Figaro* was disconcertingly, if not offputtingly, new. Even his *Die Entführung aus dem Serail* of four years earlier hadn't fully prepared them for it. *Die Entführung* is an enchanting work, and would make the reputation of any other opera composer; yet one can't wholly disagree with the sentiment expressed by the Emperor Josef II: ". . . an *extraordinary* number of notes". *Figaro* on the other hand, though a long opera, is incredibly concise. Mozart's sense of proportion, of timing, is impeccable. And within that conciseness there is a richness of musical incident and colour which had no precedent

and which for the average Viennese opera-goer was very hard to take in.

In *Figaro* Mozart achieves what he had been working towards ever since he began to write for the theatre at the age of 11: a total mastery of dramatic style, a complete language. This language incorporates the skills he had developed in the composition of instrumental music: *Figaro* comes not long after the set of six string quartets which Mozart dedicated to Haydn, and near the end of the great series of piano concertos, eight of which appeared in a period of just over a year shortly before he began working on the opera. The two worlds interact: in Mozart's hands the concerto becomes a kind of theatre, a drama carried on between piano and orchestra, while the structural principles behind the 'abstract' instrumental music are reproduced on the smaller scale of the operatic number or scene.

Mozart's consummate sense of form is a vital factor in the absolute rightness of *Figaro*. No matter how intricate the action involved nor how wide the range of emotions covered, each piece is a coherent rounded whole. And such

Ugo Benelli, Mimi Lerner, Artur Korn, William Shimell, Alberto Rinaldi, Faith Esham, Gabriele Fontana. Glyndebourne 1984

Guy Gravett

Faith Esham and Gabriele Fontana.
Glyndebourne 1984

is his mastery of large time-spans that when the drama demands a longer stretch of music – as in the great finales of Act 2 and Act 4 – he can combine as many as eight separate numbers, each a complete musical entity, into a single structure precise in its proportions, brilliant in its variety and unerring in its aptness. Music and drama are as one, moving in perfect accord.

Every element in Mozart's marvellously rich and flexible style – melody, harmony, rhythm, texture, orchestral colour – plays its part in the musical setting of the comedy. *Figaro* abounds in memorable tunes – '*Non più andrai*', '*Voi che sapete*', '*Dove sono*', Barbarina's little F minor elegy which Schubert borrowed for his piano-duet *Fantasy* in the same key, or the deliciously sly, pseudo-innocent melody to which the Countess dictates the letter which will lure the Count to his fatal rendez-vous 'under the pine-trees'. They are memorable, however, not simply because they are cat-

chy and beautiful but because they are exactly suited to the action: they embody the character, the mood, the dramatic situation. Equally important are the scraps of melody, the thematic tags which can be adapted to different shades of meaning by a composer of Mozart's ingenuity and harmonic expressiveness.

Or take the orchestration, and the unprecedented variety of instrumental combinations that Mozart employs in response to the changing demands of the drama. This is something he will take even further in *Don Giovanni* and *Così fan tutte*; it will reach its culmination in *The Magic Flute*, in which, with very few exceptions, each number has its own unique colouring. Already in *Figaro* it is remarkable. The basic orchestra of flutes, oboes, bassoons, horns and strings is used in 11 of the 45 separate movements, and the full complement, including clarinets, trumpets and drums, is deployed in the overture, at the conclusion of Acts 2 and 4 and in the march which introduces the finale of Act 3. But the remaining 30 numbers are divided between no fewer than fourteen different permutations. Among these we may note that the sensuous sound of clarinets, bassoons and horns (without oboes or flutes) is reserved for three numbers – Cherubino's '*Non sò più*', the Countess's '*Porgi, amor*' and Figaro's '*Aprite un pò quegl'occhi*', all pieces in which the characters in their different ways express their sense of being deprived of the love for which they long. Mozart's feeling for the expressive connotations of instrumental colour is an integral part of his pre-eminence as a music-dramatist. The orchestra is a leading player in the comedy.

All this, which we take for granted, was new at the time, in Italian opera at least. *Entführung* was not really a precedent, because it was a German opera; the Germans were expected to write more elaborate, 'learned' music of the sort that was quite out of place in *opera buffa*. The Italian comic operas of Mozart's rivals – Paisiello, Cimarosa, Martin y Soler, Sarti – offered nothing like it: nothing like the wealth of modulation in *Figaro*, nothing like its melodic genius or its multi-movement finales, no orchestration in the Mozartian meaning of the word, no *dramma per musica*.

The lack of these qualities – to which Mozart has accustomed us – make his contemporaries' music almost unendurably dull today. In Viennese Italian opera of the 1780s, however, such things were not considered desirable. They were defects rather than qualities: they got in the way of the comedy. *Figaro* did not do too badly at first – as an opera on Beaumarchais' notoriously subversive play *Le mariage de Figaro* (banned in the Empire) it was assured of a certain *succès de scandale* – and the simpler numbers were liked. But before long it was driven from the stage by Martin's prodigiously successful *Una cosa rara*.

Mozart had his revenge in the supper scene of *Don Giovanni*, where the band on stage plays an extract from *Una cosa rara*, together with one from Sarti's *I due litiganti*, and then puts them completely in the shade by playing '*Non più andrai*'. But *Don Giovanni* was written for the much more musical public of Prague, which had taken *Figaro* to its heart. It would be many years before Vienna did the same. Even admirers of Mozart thought he overloaded his comic operas with too much cleverness, too many restless ideas, and an excessively busy orchestration.

To us, of course, these things are among the glories of those works. They are an essential part of that complete dramatic language which Mozart created in *Figaro*. Perhaps he himself surpassed it in his later masterpieces. But *Figaro* has a special claim on our affections. *Don Giovanni* may be more haunting, *Così fan tutte* more subtle, *The Magic Flute* more beautiful (and *Idomeneo* more sublime): no opera

by Mozart, or by anyone else, has quite *Figaro's* sense of fitness, of being in total harmony with itself. None conveys the same exuberant sense of discovery – the discovery that music, while keeping within the limits of coherent, compact form, can be made to do anything and can use anything – exquisite melodies, clichés from the common operatic stock – to do it with.

It is this that makes *Figaro* the radical work it is. People have never stopped accusing da Ponte of emasculating Beaumarchais' play by removing its political teeth – as though he could ever have got the libretto accepted in Imperial Vienna if he hadn't. (As it happens, the music puts some of it back. Figaro's tirade in Act 4 of the opera may omit all reference to the class struggle, but in giving a valet an accompanied recitative – a mode of expression reserved for the upper classes – Mozart was making a very clear political point: the servant is as good as his master.) The political question, in any case, is unimportant beside

Geraint Evans. Glyndebourne 1958

Guy Gravett

145

The Paris Opera House closed by the mob, July 1789

musical utterance given to each character is his or hers alone. They inhabit an actual world, enchanted yet recognisable, companionable but full of danger.

This sense of discovery gives *Figaro* its 'electricity'. Like Jane Austen in *Pride and Prejudice* Mozart seems consciously to revel in his new mastery of the comic style. The overture celebrates it with dazzling vivacity. Unlike the overtures to *Don Giovanni*, *Così fan tutte*, *The Magic Flute*, *Entführung* and *Idomeneo* it contains no foreshadowing of the musical material of the opera; but in its mixture of energy, brilliance, mystery, and directness of melodic style, it is the ideal introduction to the drama of the *folle journée*, the 'crazy day' in the life of Count Almaviva's castle and all who live there.

We all have our favourite numbers. Mozart's, according to Michael Kelly, was the Sextet, the blissful ensemble that follows the revelation that Figaro is the long-lost illegitimate son of Bartolo and Marcellina. The music, which contrives to laugh both with and at the dramatic situation, embraces within one harmonious whole the beaming

the truly revolutionary nature of the work. In *Figaro*, for the first time, opera found the means of embodying the feelings and passions and thoughts of rounded human beings, servants and masters, as they arise in response to life. The

Artur Korn, Claudio Desderi, Hugues Cuenod, Richard Stilwell, Mimi Lerner. Glyndebourne 1984

146

*Ileana Cotrubas, Frederica von Stade
and Benjamin Luxon. Glyndebourne 1973*

delight of the unsuspecting parents, the bewilderment and irritation of the Count and his henchman the stuttering Don Curzio, the relief and high spirits of Figaro (who had come within an ace of being married off to his mother) and the sequence of sharply contrasted emotions in Susanna, from cheeky satisfaction, through amazement and outrage, to complete contentment.

In his recent book *The Mozart-da Ponte Operas* Andrew Steptoe singles out for admiring analysis the Act 1 trio 'Cosa sento', in which the Count discovers Cherubino hidden in the chair, and a single structure of irreproachable musical logic and exhilarating momentum articulates a quite complicated series of events, while giving graphic expression to the diverse feelings of the participants: the Count, by turns angry, imperious and lecherous, the leering Don Basilio, and Susanna, whose agitation is both feigned and real. It is a brilliant piece; but I would put in a strong plea for two numbers in Act 2: Susanna's G major aria 'Venite, inginocchiatevi', with its ravishing phrases for flute, oboe and bassoon and its skittish first violin part which fix the charm and vivaciousness of the character for all time; and the C major Trio 'Susanna or via sortite' which follows it, where the Count stands at the locked door of the closet and orders his wife's maid to come out, while the desperate Countess keeps her composure as best she can and Susanna, concealed in the alcove, comments breathlessly on the scene – music of

vivid harmonic and dynamic contrasts, combining powerful tension and headlong pace.

The range of emotion in *Figaro* and the variety of moods and situations encompassed are extraordinary. And beneath it all, running through this supremely felicitous comedy, the persistent Mozartian undercurrent of sadness, sensed from the outset as the curtain rises: for even while the

*Norma Burrowes, Richard Stilwell and
Isobel Buchanan. Glyndebourne 1981*

Faith Esham, Deborah Rees,
Alberto Rinaldi, Isobel Buchanan,
Richard Stilwell, Norma Burrowes.
Glyndebourne 1981

orchestra evokes with lightest touch the domesticity of the scene and the mutual affection of Figaro and Susanna, something latent in the very sweetness and simplicity of the music takes us unawares and catches at the heart. Perhaps the sadness comes partly from our recognition that life rarely attains this level of heightened awareness and intense meaningfulness. Mozart combines perfection with a sense of human longing for perfection. Shakespeare sometimes ends his comedies on the same ambiguous note. But music does not have to spell it out – Mozart's music least of all.

All the same I disagree with Nicholas Kenyon when he claims* that there is "an undeniable hollowness" in the final resolution of *Figaro*. True – if one wants to be literal – it is pretty clear that the Count's reformation is not going to outlast the night by very many hours (though he *has* knelt and publicly asked his wife's forgiveness, an astonishing gesture for so proud an aristocrat). But Figaro has got his

beloved Susanna at last; Bartolo and Marcellina have got each other – the last thing they expected, but discovering their son could conceivably be the making of both their existences; Cherubino's life lies before him, in all its excitements and disillusionments; and the Countess has given everyone an object-lesson in human charity, gentleness and large-mindedness. Mozart's reconciliations are real. They appeal to the good in human nature. He has an understanding of men and women that is Shakespearean in its psychological insight (this alone would make the mindless twit portrayed in *Amadeus* utterly implausible). His vision embraces the pain and cruelty as well as the compassion, the darkness and the light; but it is the light that he invokes.

After a good performance of *Figaro* we may all emerge, if only for an hour or two, more understanding people. And we shall certainly exclaim, with the original performers, "Viva, viva, grande Mozart".

* Mozart the ambiguous mirror,"About the House",
Christmas 1988

Curtain call with John Pritchard.
Glyndebourne 1974

The Burgtheater, Vienna

PLAYING
MOZART
HIS WAY?

PERIOD INSTRUMENTS COME
TO GLYNDEBOURNE

by Nicholas Kenyon

Twenty years ago the idea would have been a joke; ten years ago it would still have been impossible; even now it seems hard to believe. Mozart opera on period instruments at Glyndebourne is, make no mistake, a revolution, the beginning of what Simon Rattle calls a journey of discovery. This is the first time that a British opera house has put itself at the cutting edge of Mozartian performance styles, and has taken the risk of entering the currently raging debate about the use of old instruments. It is the most substantial acknowledgement yet that the revival of period instruments by the so-called 'early-music' movement, which now reaches to Berlioz and beyond, has changed the face of music-making in this country.

From one point of view, Glyndebourne is a natural place for this revolution to happen. In the 1960s the festival was an adventurous explorer of the early operatic repertory: Raymond Leppard and Peter Hall produced versions of operas by Monteverdi and Cavalli which decisively proved that these pieces could hold the operatic stage. Glyndebourne set the pace then, and the rest of the operatic world followed with enthusiasm; perhaps it will now do the same for Mozart performance in the 1990s. But from another point of view, Glyndebourne is the most surprising place in the world for a Mozartian revolution. For its Mozart style, originated by Fritz Busch and developed by other conductors, particularly John Pritchard, is a highly sophisticated creation with its roots in the Viennese tradition, based on long legato lines, sustained sound, gently moulded textures, and unobtrusive articulation. Glyndebourne's Mozart

sound – as most recently epitomized in the series of Peter Hall productions in the 1970s – has been immediately recognizable and precisely characterised.

To change this may be regarded as thoughtlessly throwing away a tradition. But Simon Rattle argues that the demands of one generation cannot be the same as those of the next ("I'd hate to think of anyone at Glyndebourne copying my style in twenty years' time") and that the moment has come for a reorientation of Mozart performing style. Rattle's interest in old instruments and early music goes back to when he was in his early twenties – a long-time friend has been the conductor and harpsichordist Nicholas Kraemer – but he says "I was not always entirely convinced by the results, and of course the actual standard of playing has improved so dramatically in the last few years". He says that the process which has led to this year's radical development actually began with the revival of *Idomeneo* which he conducted here in 1985: in fact Rattle suggests with a laugh that we may have Bernard Haitink to blame for everything that has happened since.

"Bernard asked me to do the revival and I said 'no' because I didn't think I was ready for the opera; I'd only heard it once. He collared me one day at Glyndebourne and said 'Simon, you're a fool. This is the musician's opera of all time. Go and get yourself a good recording and listen to it all before you decide.' So I went and got the Harnoncourt recording, and that absolutely opened a new world for me. Of all the other recordings I heard, none of them seemed really to gel with what was on the page. I'd

Idomeneo rehearsal at the Queen Elizabeth Hall,
August 1987: Simon Rattle with the OAE

band for the first time, it was no surprise that he chose *Idomeneo* to perform. The Orchestra of the Age of Enlightenment had been recently formed as a co-operative of London's best old-instrument players, not bound, like all the other orchestras in this field, to a single musical director. It works with very different conductors from Gustav Leonhardt to Roger Norrington, and had been anxious to persuade Rattle to direct it. So, of course, had half the other orchestras in the world; Rattle has acquired a finely honed ability to say no gracefully but definitely. Fortunately, working with period instruments was an idea whose time had come for Rattle, and he agreed. The results in the concert performances of *Idomeneo* in the Queen Elizabeth Hall in August 1987, after extensive rehearsal, persuaded everyone – including Glyndebourne – of the viability of this approach. With astonishing speed – within a couple of months – as a result in particular of the response of Peter Hall and Brian Dickie who had attended the *Idomeneo* performances, it was concluded that Rattle would use the band for his Glyndebourne Mozart series, beginning with *Figaro* this year, continuing with *Così fan tutte* in 1991 and concluding with *Don Giovanni*. The revolution was under way.

always had a problem with accepting the super-smooth de luxe approach to this sort of music. I'd been uncomfortable with the sixties Mozart style and thought I was just too young and would grow into it. But I went on and realised that I wasn't satisfied with it; the old instruments were what this music demanded."

The Nikolaus Harnoncourt recording of *Idomeneo* is not, as it happens, played on period instruments, but by the Zurich Opera orchestra which the conductor trained especially for his Mozart performances. But it demonstrates at every point an approach to texture, balance and articulation which is drawn from Harnoncourt's decades of pioneering work in the baroque and classical repertory on old instruments with his Concentus Musicus of Vienna. Attack is fierce, contrasts of *forte* and *piano* are violent, vibrato is reduced so that the impact of the dissonances is increased, phrase lengths are generally shorter, and so on. There is a directness and bite to the performance which is invigorating. It is situated exactly in the middle territory between a didactically historical approach (which both Harnoncourt and Rattle reject) and a conventional modern-style performance (which they both reject too), and articulates a distinctively contemporary response to Mozart.

Rattle was immediately taken by this approach, and when in 1987 he decided to work with a period-instrument

The development which has now led to Mozart opera on period instruments is a very long one, with its roots back in the early years of this century. Then interest in 'early music' was based on the revival of forgotten repertories, and the revival of forgotten instruments to perform those repertories. In the nineteenth century much music had been re-

Arnold Dolmetsch

150

covered and edited; it remained to bring it to life again. Arnold Dolmetsch not only wrote books on eighteenth-century interpretation but built harpsichords and played them. The lute, the viol, and the crumhorn – all of these were constructed again because there were no modern equivalents on which to perform their music. At the same time as the antiquarians were active, fiercely individualistic performers like Wanda Landowska entered the field, with thrilling performances on instruments which were not necessarily faithful in a historical sense. (She was frowned upon by the Dolmetsch camp, but her relationship with Bach was spiritual, not technological: her famous though probably apocryphal comment was "You play Bach in your way, and I will play him in his".) Later Nadia Boulanger revived Monteverdi madrigals, while in this country Julian Bream played the lute and George Malcolm the harpsichord, the beginning of a burgeoning school of brilliant old-instrument performers who were in no sense confined by history.

In the years after the Second World War a second development began to occur – not the revival of forgotten music on forgotten instruments, but the transformation of performance style in music we all thought we knew well. This was much more of a challenge and indeed (to some) a threat; Harnoncourt and Leonhardt, August Wenzinger, Frans Brüggen and others, in an enormously influential series of recordings, began to change our notion of how Bach and the baroque repertory could sound. Slowly, this interacted with a response to the new, small-scale performing styles on modern instruments of Neville Marriner, Raymond Leppard and others, to bring about a sea-change in our attitude to baroque performance. Symphony orchestras suddenly began to shy away from the Brandenburgs, and Hamilton Harty's *Water Music* was, sadly for many, abandoned in the search for Handel's own stylistic current.

These two strands in early music performance can be seen as intertwining around the end of the 1960s, when the movement really acquired its huge popular following. David Munrow was bursting upon the scene with his concerts of unmatchable vitality and enthusiasm, bringing forgotten music and curious medieval instruments out of the scholar's backroom and onto the concert platform, where they held their own against all competition. On record, Nikolaus Harnoncourt was performing Bach's B minor Mass with vivid conviction using old instruments, boys' voices, and light textures, and making a stirring (if extreme) declaration in his notes for the recording: "An interpretation must be attempted in which the entire romantic tradition of performance is ignored . . . the attempt must be made to hear and perform [these pieces] as

if they had never been interpreted before, as though they had never been formed nor distorted."

The idea that what Jonathan Miller would call the "subsequent performances" of a masterwork were a form of distortion was quick to take root. Musicians talked of "getting back to the original performance", "cleaning the dirt from the painting"; exact performing forces were recreated and the precise form of Handel's *Messiah* on a certain date was followed to the last deleted bar. Looking back, I think that sheer enthusiasm for the sound of these performances – the revelations of their light, airy textures, clear, crisp timbres and transparent articulation – tended to overcome worries about what was actually happening in attempts to recreate history. By the mid-1970s we had period-instrument orchestras in London formed by Christopher Hogwood, Roger Norrington and Trevor Pinnock, and we were beginning to lead the world in this area of activity. By the time the *Water Music* and *Messiah* reached the Proms around 1980, the bandwagon was well and truly rolling.

It is perhaps strange that at this time a stronger attack was not mounted on the basis of the movement. Those professional musicians (and there were plenty of them) who loathed period instruments tended not to dispute their claim to be 'authentic'. They disputed the arrogance of the performers (the claim that theirs was the only way to play) and their competence, points with which at that time it was easy to agree. As it happened, one of the few strong objections in print to the claims of the movement appeared in this programme book in 1984, when Raymond Leppard laid into those who claimed "that the actual playing of these specialised instruments is the only way for this music to be performed . . . It is then that we enter the world of cult and bigotry that is as offensive to the art of music as it is inhibiting and unattractive at a human level." He did not argue with players' taking up old playing techniques, but he did go so far as to assert that "many of them who take this *droict chemin* do so because their road must, otherwise, be very stony" – an accusation of sheer unprofessionalism which was typical of many musicians' views on the subject. Leppard has expanded and partly modified his views in his recently published short book *Authenticity in Music*.*

As playing standards rapidly improved, however, such accusations became less frequent. Period instrument players had to re-invent a performance style from scratch, as it were, and in the absence of subsidy enabling them to do it in private there was arguably too much public exposure too quickly. But that also enabled the vast improvements both in the instruments themselves and in the playing standards which are now evident. It also enabled things to move

* Faber Music, 1988.

forward chronologically. As instrument builders found ever more demand for their work, it was possible to move on from reproducing baroque oboes to classical oboes, from flutes of 1750 to flutes of 1780 or 1800, and new possibilities opened up. From Handel on old instruments it was but a small step to J C Bach *ditto*, and thence to Mozart.

But how are the classical instruments that will be used in this *Figaro* different from their modern equivalents? A frequent source of puzzlement is that any number of distinguished violinists claim to use a Stradivarius instrument – isn't this an 'original'? No, it isn't, for all Stradivari violins (except for a precious few in museums) were modified and altered when concert halls became bigger and the need for more volume and more projection became acute. Fingerboards were lengthened and their angle to the body of the instrument changed. Bridges became higher, strings were wound in metal instead of being simply made of gut. The design of the bow was changed completely so that greater attack, off-the-string bowing, and many other new effects were possible. Analagous changes took place in other string instruments – cellos began to use spikes, for example, which helped firmness and attack but arguably removed flexibility and poise – while the changes in the woodwind family were even more radical. There is a tendency to look at all these changes as technological improvements, and to say 'wouldn't Mozart have been delighted with them!' But the technological advances served new repertory: in the woodwind they are partly connected with the desire for

The Drottningholm Court Theatre

greater sophistication in chromatic fingerings which is relevant to nineteenth-century music but not to Mozart. And they result in radical changes of character and inflection, making the modern instruments richer in harmonics, capable of many special effects, but losing the essential simplicity and tonal directness of the eighteenth-century original. These instruments were not inadequate old versions of modern instruments, they were essentially different. Their textures and timbres are not the be-all and end-all of period-style performance. But they put before us the kinds of sounds with which the composer worked, and for modern players and audiences they help in escaping the preconceptions of two centuries of developing tradition, enabling us to look and hear afresh. The instruments are only the beginning of the process of recovering an approach to articulation, bowing, vibrato, rhythm and tempi which reflects that of the eighteenth century, but they are a vital – and, to many, a wonderfully attractive and revelatory – part of that process.

A history of Mozart performance style remains to be written; it will be a fascinating exercise. I can remember precisely the record which converted me to Mozart on period instruments: an account of the Oboe Quartet played by Michel Piguet on Telefunken, made years ago and played with a lightness, delicacy and graceful passion that was totally disarming. Then there were some pioneering accounts of the string quartets by Jaap Schröder's Esterhazy Quartet. But the project that really began to create a Mozartian style on old instruments in this country was Christopher Hogwood's complete recording of the symphonies for Oiseau-Lyre in the years after 1980: a major instance of record-company patronage making possible the development of a style. (In the event its investment must have been repaid many times with the huge popular success of this series, which entered the Billboard charts in the United States next to Pavarotti.)

At the same time there have been many other, widely different, attempts to interpret Mozart with period instruments: very early on, Roger Norrington performed the Requiem and earlier this year he made *Die Zauberflöte* the focus of a weekend on the South Bank; John Eliot Gardiner has been making strongly profiled recordings of the symphonies and of the piano concertos with Malcolm Bilson and his English Baroque Soloists, and now Frans Brüggen's Orchestra of the Eighteenth Century has produced some highly sophisticated Mozart symphony performances. Operatically, *Die Zauberflöte* was staged some years ago at the Holland Festival using old instruments with only limited success; much more significantly, at Drottningholm in Sweden, in the perfectly preserved eighteenth-century theatre there, Arnold Östman has been creating a very

Period instruments played by members of the OAE

153

interesting Mozart operatic tradition with period instruments, and the results have recently become more widely available in the Oiseau-Lyre recordings of *Così fan tutte* and *Le nozze di Figaro*. The way forward is wide open for these old resources to be used to create a new vision of Mozart.

Simon Rattle approaches *Figaro* without any illusions about historical faithfulness. Like many practitioners in this area, Rattle totally rejects the notion that he is recreating anything from the past by using old instruments. "I'm frankly not very interested in the archaeological side, and talking about being faithful to history just sets me off. . . . The whole idea of the 'original' is so problematical and suspect. But if we can follow what we know to have been Mozart's intentions, this has to mean something. It's a way of getting closer to the music. Every age has got to do this for itself, and it is now a matter which is simply too pressing; the style has to be re-thought and to do the opposite and just accept the Glyndebourne style would for me be a terrible cop-out."

But once embarked on, a new style is a great commitment. Rattle quotes Harnoncourt as saying that "you don't realise you're in a boat until you push away from the harbour", and that is what the experience of this *Figaro* will be like for all concerned. "It's the first time in living memory the parts have been marked up in October for rehearsals the following June!", he adds: Rattle has worked closely with the leader of the band, Roy Goodman, to get the articulations and the phrasings right. And they will have been tried out with modern instruments as well, for Rattle will have given two concert performances of the opera with his City of Birmingham Symphony Orchestra in March this year.

Rattle emphasises that he doesn't feel with old instruments as if he's restricting himself: "It gives more freedom to be expressive, and a great deal is actually easier on the old instruments. However you use modern instruments, there's always a feeling that you have to scale it down for Mozart, so you're always slightly counterfeiting. The great thing with old instruments is that the passion and energy which so often one felt the need to inhibit can be expressed with full force, and you're always within the style. That's a marvellous result. It solves a lot of problems with the sheer physical and emotional expression in the piece."

The same problem, Rattle feels, applies to the voices – and that has a lot to do with matters of tempo which a study of performing practice can get right. "One of the reasons there are so few people around who can sing the Countess is that all her music's been taken at half speed for so long. So you need someone who can sing the Strauss *Four Last Songs*! And that's just wrong. She is a young woman, and the idea of '*Dove sono*' as a real dramatic voyage of someone from despair to discovery – this is just not something which comes across in most performances with that drifting, beautiful sound."

There will be many more such experiments to be tried, interpretations to be re-thought, before this *Figaro* comes to the stage. Open ears and fresh minds will be the only requirements for enjoying it. And Glyndebourne may be in for some surprises: the instruments play at eighteenth-century pitch, so some of the rehearsal pianos have been re-tuned. . . . In answer to the inevitable question as to whether Rattle will carry his old-instrument exploration forward into the nineteenth century as others have done, he is (for once) cautious: "You'll have to give me time . . .".

Simon Rattle

DESERVING CAUSES

by Rodney Milnes

It's as well to be reminded that *Arabella* was once considered shocking. I remember the well-scrubbed, tweedy lady in charge of the university record library doing what she doubtless considered her moral duty when I sought to borrow the first LP of extracts from the opera: "Oh dear me no, *not* a very nice opera," she said. "We were all very keen on *Rosenkavalier* and *Ariadne* when they came out, but shocked when Strauss wrote *Fräulein Arabella*. Didn't like it

Lisa Della Casa as Arabella

at all. Rather mucky, we thought." (I don't know where the royal 'we' came from, or what occasioned the uncanonical *Fräulein* – sarcasm perhaps.) The LP extracts concentrated on the romantic numbers, of course, and ignored the naughty bits, but it didn't take long to root them out. An (at best) anonymous or (at scarcely better) mistaken-identity act of copulation as the dramatic pivot of a social comedy may well have been thought shocking then, and remains slightly sordid, if not trivial, now. I saw *Arabella* soon after, and two things remain vividly in the mind: the vocal and physical beauty of the young Lisa Della Casa, and the elderly Mandryka's gleaming black toupee, which bore no resemblance to human hair and must surely have led an independent life of its own. For the thirty years that have since passed I have enjoyed a love-hate relationship with the opera that is long overdue for resolution.

Does Mandryka deserve Arabella? Surely not: a man who can go through a 180 degree emotional about-turn on the strength of an overheard conversation deserves little more than to be told to grow up. Does the haughty, self-assured Arabella deserve Mandryka? Probably, and serve her right. Does Matteo deserve Zdenka? Hardly: someone who thinks that all life's problems can be solved by the above-mentioned brief, anonymous act, instantly tries to lie his way out of it, and then takes on board gender confusion without turning very many hairs deserves to see a good doctor (Freud was not, alas, practising in Vienna as early as 1860). But then no one deserves Zdenka, one of the most beautiful characters in all dramatic literature (or a silly and misguided young woman, depending on how you look at

155

these things). One wishes her well, albeit nervously.

More important, does *Arabella* deserve its status as the most popular of the problem-ridden post-World-War-1 Strauss operas, operas whose problems Glyndebourne has done so much to dispel? Is not the whole love-at-first-sight, Mr Right framework and the glutinous Happy End more suited to the world of Mills and Boon than to that of 20th century opera? Are we really supposed to become involved with these four characters in the grip of irrational erotic obsession, for all the world as if they were taking part in some nightmare bourgeois version of *Turandot*? Doesn't the traditional musical language and structure of *Arabella* represent a backward step in the context of the technical advances of *Intermezzo*? Can even the most fervent Strauss-fancier deny that for a dangerous twenty minutes in the second act the composer is on auto-pilot? Or deny that in the same act the drama momentarily loses its way?

The structural problems, whether they be admitted or not, have two causes. First, the untimely death of Hugo von Hofmannsthal in 1929. He had just finished final revisions to the first act of the libretto, and Strauss's telegram of congratulations arrived after the poet had succumbed to a heart attack on the day of his elder son's funeral. The other two acts remained unrevised, and Strauss set them as they stood as an act of piety. Simply as a piece of exposition, the first act is one of the most perfect things Strauss and Hofmannsthal achieved together; the resolution in the third act is on the same level, but all too often disfigured by 'traditional' and massively insensitive cuts; it is the development in the second act that remains worrying, mainly because Zdenka and Matteo fade from sight. One of their exchanges is even set in tandem with a less than earth-shakingly important conversation for Adelaide and Mandryka, and in general the producer has to show considerable ingenuity to keep them in the dramatic foreground. But then the imbalance between the two couples, or rather the lopsided quadrilateral – Arabella and Matteo and Mandryka, plus Zdenka – was part of the process of the adaptation from the original source, adaptation that surely would have been concluded more smoothly had Hofmannsthal lived.

The source was *Lucidor* a short-story sketch written by Hofmannsthal in 1910 and subtitled 'Characters for an Unwritten Comedy'. Save for Arabella, all these characters have different names, which need not concern us here. Adelaide is a widow, greatly impoverished, as in the opera. The elder daughter Arabella, her mother thinks, is 'lacking in feeling', whereas Zdenka is feeling personified. Zdenka caught typhus aged eleven and had her hair cropped; she is painfully shy and prefers riding astride, so her disguise as

a boy is thus both economically desirable and a natural progression. Besides, there is a mysterious bachelor uncle out of whom Adelaide hopes to wheedle money, and the old misogynist is fond of little Zdenko, who is sent to visit him regularly. Matteo is rich and noble; he too is liked by the bachelor uncle, and as in the opera he is hopelessly, though less hysterically, in love with Arabella. Arabella will have none of him, and flirts with a Tyrolean gentleman farmer mainly to annoy him (the Tyrolean, mentioned only in passing, becomes Mandryka in the opera).

Matteo's relationship with Zdenko/Zdenka is more developed than that suggested in the opera; they often go out riding together and sometimes visit the uncle. Matteo's frustrated love, much discussed on the rides, leads Zdenka to write her first letter under Arabella's name, confessing her love but warning Matteo not to expect any outward change. The satisfaction for Zdenka lies both in being able to express her own love for Matteo and in seeing him happy. For his part Matteo, the upright officer and repressed romantic, rather enjoys the inexplicable existence of 'two' Arabellas, the passionate letter-writer and the cool, aloof girl with whom he has formal social relations.

He enjoys it even more when the letter-writer takes him to bed – he and Zdenka sleep together regularly, not just once, as in the opera – and the contrast between the day-time Arabella, so assured, unfeeling and cynical, and the night-time Arabella, so submissive and passionate, intrigues him ever more. The colder the daytime Arabella grows, the more cheerfully Matteo enters into what he sees as a game, a game that could be played indefinitely were it not for the mother's sudden decision to leave Vienna. Zdenka writes Arabella's letter of farewell, Matteo confronts the daytime Arabella with her night-time activities, and the embarrassing conversation is interrupted by the appearance and confession of Zdenka. She and Matteo are left alone, and the sketch ends with the words: 'Life may create the dialogue that followed, comedy might try to imitate it, but a story cannot.' Music, however, could.

But music chose not to. If *Arabella* is shocking, the action of *Lucidor* put on stage as it stands would be unacceptably so to a society that had banned Schnitzler's *Reigen* and much of Wedekind. One bout of love-making might be tolerated, but several, so calculatedly undertaken, would not. A pity, since the sharp contrast between the two sisters, one selfish and aloof, the other so generous, so giving, so selfless that she chooses to be someone else, is as promising as the basic idea of how we perceive each other, of how (brushing aside details of gender) friends become lovers, how enemies *are* lovers, how appearances seem both everything and

First production at Glyndebourne, 1984

Guy Gravett

nothing. Interestingly enough, *Lucidor* has since been adapted as a ballet.

The correspondence between Strauss and Hofmannsthal shows how, step by step and at Strauss's insistence, the material was adapted; how the Tyrolean farmer became the Balkan landowner, how Arabella's character was gradually softened, how these two became the protagonists and how Zdenka and Matteo were pushed into the background. Even the penultimate draft of the first act ended with Zdenka's promise to Matteo of one more letter, a scene now placed earlier in the act and replaced by Arabella's monologue. Few Straussians would complain about that, but as many might want a corresponding adjustment made in the second act to bring the second – hitherto first – couple back into prominence. For Zdenka is one of the most immediately attractive of all Hofmannsthal's embodiments of the principle of self-sacrifice in the cause of what is right – Elektra's sacrifice of her femininity, the Marschallin's of her lover, and Ariadne's, the Empress's and Helena's of their lives. The last three are rewarded with something other than death, just as Zdenka is cheated of her enchantingly

daffy promise of suicide. Zdenka, with her matchless beauty of spirit, deserves to be centre stage, and deserves her Matteo. One prays he will be worthy of her.

If a determined prosecuting counsel could make mince-meat of the second act of the opera as it stands (on paper that is – a clever producer can render its shortcomings comparatively insignificant), the third plays into the defence's hands – always assuming it isn't cut to ribbons. Opera makes a habit of testing human love, of passing it through the furnace to see if it will emerge tempered and ever stronger. The furnace blazes fiercely in the third act of *Arabella*. Post-coital conversations are a bit of a trial at the best of time, but the one here, in which one partner thinks this is what it is while the other knows jolly well that it isn't, is especially painful. Audiences should not be required to witness such events. When the rest of the cast arrives the innocent Arabella unwittingly puts her foot in it time after time, reinforcing Mandryka's lunatic suspicions. As the imbroglio grows ever more bleak, one is grateful for one of Hofmannsthal's more inspired acts of *Stimmungsbrechung* – Waldner calling for his pistols, which are of course in hock. I have seen performances of the opera in which the tension engendered by this non-communication on an epic scale, tension screwed so tight that music can no longer contain it and dialogue has to take over, has become so intense that I had completely forgotten what happened next. Never has the appearance of the pathetic *deus/dea ex machina* been so welcome.

Was jetzt noch kommt? A lot. Characteristically, Strauss saw the absolute necessity for a new musical idea to express Mandryka's right and proper remorse, something to add to thematic material that, however dextrously manipulated, has been more or less constant since the first act: the new musical idea is heard most insistently in his short solo before the finale. That tempering remorse saves him from a *fatuité* bordering on that of Escamillo. Matteo is subjected to one of the briskest shotgun weddings in opera, and his acceptance can seem too-good-to-be-true to the point of inconsequentiality. But there is one cut still made even in 'complete' *Arabellas*, a pair of lines for Matteo that add a necessary perspective: 'It was too dark in the room, I didn't hear your voice – and yet it's as though I suspected it all along, my sweet little Zdenko' (amateur psychologists should note the male ending). I assume the cut is still made on grounds of taste.

Just as Mandryka is saved by his remorse, so is Arabella by the way she unquestioningly stands by her sister and later admits that she has been taught a lesson: 'You are the better of us two, you have the more loving heart. . . . Thank you for teaching me that we shouldn't want things, or long

157

for them, weigh them up or stint on them, but only give and love for ever.' Those words are also sometimes cut.

What is Arabella to be saved from? I once remember an experienced critic writing that he found soprano X's Arabella too cold and distant. So do her mother and sister. The first thing we hear about Arabella is her mother saying that she is as proud as she is beautiful, sentiments soon to be capped by Zdenka, who to Arabella's face calls her 'proud, flirtatious, and cold into the bargain'. In the process of development from the subsidiary character in *Lucidor* into the sympathetic protagonist of the opera, Arabella has retained a significant amount of her former self: she is an enormously complex creature. The self-possession, the coolness and the command are forced upon a young girl quite unfairly: she has been made aware that the salvation of her dotty family lies in her hands – she is responsible for them all and she is to be sold to the highest bidder. In the first version of Act 1 there is a question of her being married off ('mated', *verkuppelt*, in her own bitter words) to a rich building contractor, a man 'in trade' ('over my dead body' replies Adelaide). An element of her cynical fatalism survives in the present first act: 'perhaps I shall have to take him' – Elemer, the most obvious candidate.

Is her responsibility for the family the reason for her ending her relationship with Matteo, who in the opera is impoverished, not rich and well-born, and so ruled out as a contender in the marriage market? Arabella admits that she might have loved him once, but it's over, just as she admits that she can quickly become fond of a man and as quickly lose interest. She has a practised coolness and command when dealing with importunate men, even with Mandryka at the beginning of the second act until she is swept off her feet by his ardour. She is coolly in command of the situation as she dismisses the three suitors; perhaps her coolness and poise deserve the trials of the third act. Maybe yes, maybe no, but the dark side to her, the irritability an

impatience with those less clever, make her so much more than the vapid heroine of a romantic novel, a woman seen in the round, a true Strauss-and-Hofmannsthal creation.

Which is of course why *Arabella* deserves its special status. The characters are drawn in such depth by librettist and composer that, as in *Rosenkavalier*, we seem to know both their pre- and their post-history: Mandryka, the fabulously rich, half-peasant provincial landowner, impulsive, unthinking, generous to a fault (I wager his first wife was a submissive ninny); Waldner, the cavalry officer fallen on hard times, but one who can still muster some shreds of dignity when the family honour is impugned; Adelaide, described in *Lucidor* as 'a madwoman, but of the more likeable kind', and just that, one of the silliest and most intensely lovable mothers I know, and good for her, say I, that when she gets her daughter off her hands she's ready for a fling with one of the ex-boyfriends; poor, crazed Matteo – have not all of us in the dim, distant past suffered the agonies of unrequited love and dare we deny an iota of fellow-feeling? A canny producer, as at Glyndebourne, can work with canny singers and turn the three Counts into three-dimensional characters, and do the same with the much-abused Fiakermilli – abused by critics as regularly as she is by Mandryka. People want to sing these roles, and people want to hear them sung.

As in all Hofmannsthal's librettos, there are ideas of indescribably poetic truth and beauty. The image of the glass of water as pledge of undying love surpasses even the silver rose, and how economically Strauss matches it musically with little more than a chord of B flat major. Even the Mills and Boon love-at-first sight content is given resonance by poetic distancing: Mandryka falls in love with a portrait, and proposes solemnly in the words of his late uncle, who would never have been so solemn, just as Zdenka is forced to voice her own feelings and arrange the fateful assignation in the third person, as someone else.

Production photographs by Guy Gravett of the first performances at Glyndebourne, 1984

There are uncomfortable little truths that cannot but strike a hideous chord, like Mandryka's opening gambit of court-ship, which is to talk glowingly about his dead wife (hardly tactful, and understandably ill-received) or Arabella's inevitably expressed hope that she and Elemer can remain 'good friends' (equally ill-received). We've all done that. And sticky moments are bitter-sweetly defused: Arabella's sightings of the handsome stranger in the street outside are, again, the stuff of romantic novels, but the second time, when she remarks upon his great big soulful eyes, she has her little sister to bring her down to earth and ask what she means: he wasn't even looking up. No, he wasn't. They never do in real life.

But it is not poetic images, rather musical ones that draw people into the opera house, and it is the music that has won *Arabella* its special status in the Strauss canon. Not just the big moments, the finales to the outer acts and the love duet, in which Strauss pursues both his well-known love affair with the soprano voice and his firm, no-nonsense friendship with the baritone of the species. For all the comparative conservatism of technique, that technique is here fielded with easy, fluent mastery. Characterization through music is subtly economic: How striking the con-trast between healthy, bluff, ever-so-slightly boring dia-tonic Elemer and the chromatically tormented Matteo, and how interesting that the latter's feverish chromaticisms should briefly invade the equally diatonic world of Man-dryka, at the moment he is describing his convalescence after an unfortunate encounter with a she-bear. The crum-bling world of the Waldners is suggested by the simplest of means, the wholesome purity of Zdenka with a just sufficient undercurrent of elusive chromatic yearning. The whole score spanks along at near-conversational pace, and is so cleverly orchestrated that the words are always aud-ible. The manipulation, the constant development of the kaleidoscopically shifting thematic material is of the sort that we praise inordinately in Janáček but take for granted in Strauss, who was of course too successful, too soon, for his own good.

What is it, precisely, that is developed? In much literary opera, opera in which musical gestures are associated with more or less specific dramatic ideas or people, you can tell – certainly in Wagner up to the end of *Rheingold* or Strauss up to most of *Frau ohne Schatten* – that this music represents Giants and that music represents Unborn Children. But try as you may, the handful of themes associated with Arabella herself, let alone the supporting cast, defy specific labelling. It would be nice to be able to say – and people have tried – that this theme is the daytime Arabella, and that one the night-time, yet once you think you have worked the difference out, Strauss eludes you with a cross-reference or a shifting development that scurries off in quite a different direction: it is tempting to call *Arabella* the most symphonic of Strauss's operas.

The character of Arabella herself, then, defies analysis as much as her music does. She is a figure of mystery, or unattainability, always just beyond your grasp. Neither Arabella nor *Arabella* can be pinned down, which is why I love them both so much. Almost as much as I love Zdenka.

Hofmansthal and Strauss

W. Bithorn

159

Hogarth

THE RAKE —
A PROGRESS

by John Cox

Ever since its world premiere in Venice in 1951 the history of *The Rake's Progress* has been inextricably bound up with Glyndebourne. The production was entrusted to Carl Ebert, Glyndebourne's Artistic Director, with the intention that he should reproduce it here soon afterwards. In the event, this was only partially realised because nobody liked the original designs, so that when Glyndebourne first presented *Rake* at the Edinburgh Festival of 1953, it was furnished with a completely new visual concept by Osbert Lancaster. At the time, and for at least two more decades, Lancaster was famous principally for his front page cartoon in the *Daily Express* peopled with characterful portraits of the British upper class, old and new, whom he observed with a sharply satirical eye but also with a rueful affection. The production was an unexpected success and while *The Rake's Progress* had trouble maintaining a foothold in the operatic repertoire elsewhere, at Glyndebourne it was able to be presented in five out of eleven seasons up to 1963. Much of the credit for this must go to Lancaster, whose colourful and witty designs helped to sugar the pill of a 'difficult' score and a complex libretto.

In considering Glyndebourne's second production of this opera which I directed in the mid-70s, the supreme importance of design was a forgone conclusion – yet Lancaster himself had not been principally a stage designer, or indeed a painter. He was a satirical cartoonist in a worthy English tradition reaching back to none other than William Hogarth himself, the originator of a series of paintings called *A Rake's Progress*, which Stravinsky had first seen at a loan exhibition in Chicago, and which Hogarth had turned into a series of even more famous etchings.

It so happened that a prominent young English artist had, ten years before, also etched a series called *A Rake's Progress*, based on his own picaresque career in the United States. David Hockney, like Hogarth, unlike Lancaster, was also a painter, but at that time his drawings and graphics played a much more important part in his high profile reputation, not least his *Rake's Progress*, with its cool irony and, albeit self-directed, satire. I felt sure that, whatever else I might want my production to look like, it must have strong outline and sympathetic humour. There was enough evidence that Hockney would provide this, so with the approval of Glyndebourne's top brass, I approached him with the project.

His initial response was cautious. The opera at that point evidently held no great appeal to him and he was worried about his technical competence. I reassured him of the quality and dedication of the Glyndebourne craftsmen, and urged him to get to know the piece a bit better before saying no. My own input at this stage was to say that I wanted to tell the tale clearly, with a certain detachment, without however sacrificing the potential emotional impact. I pointed out that within the three-act structure the authors had asked for three scenes on a sort of A B A formula, whereby either the two outer scenes would be large and the inner one small, or vice versa, to enable scenes to be prepared in groups and facilitate quick changes. I made no historical or geographical stipulations, and confidently expected him to propose something daringly modern.

Thus I was quite unprepared for his desire to locate the design uncompromisingly in the style and content of Hogarth's own graphics, with a vigorous application of the

160

William Hogarth The Orgy, *from*
The Rake's Progress *1732/3*

Costume designs by David Hockney © 1975

etching technique known as cross hatching – and a severely restricted palette of three colours which could serve to make the results strikingly his own. He was to say later in the catalogue to *Hockney Paints the Stage** that "the paramount task is to interpret the composer's ideas – to find an equivalent in form and colour for the music". To my ear and eye, this is what he had done.

The colour coding was simple and effective. In the opening scene of innocence green was predominant, with some blue. The only red was the startling splash of Tom's jacket—a small, concentrated spot which was to spread and bleed everywhere with the onset of luxury and success – emphatic and profuse in the brothel scene, no less prevalent but ordered in his grand London house. Apart from Nick Shadow, black arrives significantly for the first time with Baba's Sedan chair, and this is the fulcrum around which

* Thames and Hudson, 1983

his fortune turns. All her possessions are black or black and white, and his rejection of her leads finally to his undoing, when all colour departs the scene. His damnation is suitably the blackest scene of all – modelled by Hockney in black card with white incisions. Finally, in Bedlam, as Tom goes quietly and sweetly mad, comes the tenderest use of all three colours in equal measure, with very little black and a great deal of white – a catharsis.

As for the content of the scenes, for the first I asked for a garden of strict classical purity with a wall in preference to a fence, and a solid door. For to Tom the countryside, because it presents no opportunities, is a prison. He, however, cannot open the door. Only Nick and Anne have the

resolution necessary to do so. The swing was for me a necessity – it is something of a musical pun as well as a symbol in 18th century painting of innocence under siege.

Hockney had the cynical idea of putting one in the brothel, too, put to a far baser use, but sadly the amount of flown scenery packed into the flytower for other shows denied us the necessary space. The brothel is the scene of Tom's loss of innocence, just as the madhouse is where he, insane, regains it. I asked for these scenes to be related visually, which they are. Both feature a bed centre stage on which these events take place – the one a setting for his amoral catechism to his 'Lady Bishop' (sic), Mother Goose, the other for his penitential confession to his 'Venus', Anne Trulove. I also feel strongly that there is no eroticism in the music of the brothel scene. The customers and whores alike all behave with a rowdy naivety reminiscent of children. Hockney provided me with a kind of grown ups' nursery with toy-cupboards instead of bedrooms. A motto hanging overhead invoked the cartoonist's privilege of adding text to illustration.

The second act is concerned only with Tom's house, inside and outside. His name and proud new title, blazoned over the front door, sustain the idea of text, while for both Tom and his new wife Baba the outward sign of worldly success is the formation of a collection, in his case somewhat slyly, of pictures. Art, too, has its part to play in the spendthrift economy, satisfying an urge not unremoved from gluttony. Echoing Hogarth, but also much of his own early work, Hockney framed the interiors with curtains, another device for detachment and parenthesis in amplification of the cross

Costume design by David Hockney © 1975

hatching technique which in these scenes acquires its richest variety. Another striking feature of these interiors is the lack of any door in the designs. Since no one enters except the Devil, the idea of his insinuating himself into the picture via its frame was pleasing.

163

The death of colour and the onset of black as the key to Act 3 has already been referred to – Baba, Anne and the Auctioneer 'survive' in colour. In the graveyard we again rejected the stage description provided by the authors in favour of a direct Hogarthian reference to *The Idle 'Prentice* – in any case an altogether more neo-classical setting for the long *recitativo secco* adapted by Stravinsky from *opera seria*.

For Bedlam, Hockney restored colour and raised text to its highest importance in a wild profusion of graffiti. At first he proposed five or six lunatics standing in little pens, but from this we evolved the most extreme design proposition of the production – the chorus, not as fellow madmen but as figments of Tom's diseased mind, talking to him, taunting him and finally uttering his own threnody. I didn't want a genre scene with a lot of private 'Actors Studio' insanity

© *David Hockney*

scattering the focus of the scene. The action comes full circle here, via the brothel back to the garden where Tom first paid court to Anne in pastoral style. The motionless, indifferent masks secure an unchallenged choral backdrop for their ruined love and his quiet extinction.

The designs are by no means 'modern' in the sense of seeking new technical ways of presenting a work. The scenery is painted on canvas flats, cloths and borders. It stands up or hangs in the time-honoured way. If an object or a piece of furniture is not to be used it is painted two dimensionally onto the scenery, if it must be three dimensional, its surfaces are decorated into the scheme of things.

Yet in many different ways they challenged the Glyndebourne craft departments to the limits. For the scenery Hockney did not produce sketches, but insisted on making models. He chose a small scale for these, applying the cross hatching with the utmost care so that colour, thickness of line and spacing had not to be 'interpreted' in the scene shop, but accurately translated on the full size scenery. It was a mind-boggling, eye-crossing task, carried out to Hockney's total satisfaction by Stephen Jetten and his staff at Harker's Studios in Walworth.

Guy Gravett

As for the costumes, we had to print all our own fabrics in order to reproduce the design concept. Silk-screens were made and we went to Glyndebourne in dead of winter and tried out all the colours, crossed and recrossed, square, oblong, trapezoid, rhomboid, all to look as if they had been applied with pens onto a white or black base. Hockney tested the viability of each by standing at the front and the back of the theatre in turn until he was satisfied that each combination 'read' as shading as well as pattern. Tony Ledell, the Wardrobe Manager, was then faced with the colossal task of printing all the fabrics required, from the simplest cottons to the heaviest wools, and combining them to the best advantage in conjunction with Hockney's drawings and references to create the costumes. His contribution was crucial.

Tony Ledell,
Wardrobe Manager

Guy Gravett

Detail from plate 9 of The Rake's
Progress by William Hogarth

Perhaps the trickest task of realisation, however, was the hair. When we tried wigs made from natural hair we could not obtain the strength of colour or line provided by the drawings, so that everything looked 'designed' except the heads. Sheila Dunsdon, the Wig Mistress, eventually came up with the excellent proposal of using the waxed thread manufactured for making the wig base itself, forming it into wigs. She found a factory in Ulster which produced it in colour and bought up the entire stock shortly before it went out of business. The subsequent use of lampshade fringe in Milan and San Francisco has been nowhere near as good.

We found that, while it was possible to stylise the make-up through colour, it was not possible to carry the principle of cross hatching onto the faces without obliterating expression.

In other words, in spite of the traditional form of the designs, the treatment of their surface detail demanded quite innovative solutions, so that they offer a completely fresh way of looking at the stage for those with willing eyes. For the scenes are not so much represented as illustrated, demanding of the spectator a more continuous and engaged visual response to the events which the scenes and characters present.

Does this challenge the music and the drama for attention in an indiscrete way? I believe not. Hockney's style here is of a spare neo-classicism which perfectly matches the musical style Stravinsky adopts for the opera, while Auden and Kallman's artfully simple emblematic parable is strongly assisted by the steely strength of line.

In the 1954 Glyndebourne programme, Eric Blom writes of Stravinsky ". . . if we want the simple truth, we can still do him ample justice by declaring that he was exactly the right composer for this opera. For it is an opera quite deliberately made artificial, and the musician required for it had above all else to be an artificer, a master craftsman, a stylist. Stravinsky is these things, *mutatis mutandis*, as Mozart was, with the difference that Mozart brought all his life's experience, artistic and human, within an impeccable style of his own, whereas Stravinsky delights in essays of a great variety of styles." *Mutatis mutandis* also Hockney, who settled on a style which feels absolutely right for the job.

Fifteen years is not an exceptional life span for an opera production. It is not the oldest still in the Glyndebourne store and is positively adolescent compared with some still at Covent Garden. However, the fact remains that when this production was first done in 1975 we could have had no idea of its world wide destiny. Glyndebourne's own production has been seen during six seasons at most of its principal English touring venues, and in Angers, Bremen, Paris and Nancy. It was re-created in larger format for La Scala Milan and presented also in Genoa before being

purchased by San Francisco Opera. They in turn have more than covered their costs by renting to New York, Dallas, Toronto, Honolulu and Vancouver. The television recording from Glyndebourne is available on video cassette, while the models played a prominent part in the exhibition *Hockney Paints the Stage* in Minneapolis, Mexico City, Ontario, Chicago, Fort Worth, San Francisco and London.

In short, there can be no doubt that once again a Glyndebourne production has secured the position of Stravinsky's *Rake's Progress* near the centre of the standard operatic repertoire; and again it is the contribution of a major painter which has ensured this – not inappropriately, surely for an opera born of a picture in the first place.

David Hockney on the set with Stage Management,
Technical and Stage staff

'An Independent Draughtsman'
by William Hogarth

Stravinsky by Jean Cocteau

Guy Gravett

Anthony Whitworth-Jones
General Administrator

Stephen Markeson

Sir Peter Hall CBE
Artistic Director
Director: *A Midsummer Night's
Dream, Le nozze di Figaro*
1970, 71, 74 *La Calisto*
1972, 73, 79 *Il ritorno d'Ulisse in
patria*
1973, 74, 76, 81, 84 *Le nozze di
Figaro*
1977, 78, 82, 86 *Don Giovanni*
1978, 79, 84, 87 *Così fan tutte*
1979, 81 *Fidelio*
1981, 84, 86 (Hong Kong) *A
Midsummer Night's Dream*
1982 *Orfeo ed Euridice*
1984, 86 *L'incoronazione di Poppea*
1985, 87 *Carmen*
1985, 86 *Albert Herring*
1986 *Simon Boccanegra*
1987, 88 *La traviata*
1988 *Falstaff*

Andrew Davis
Musical Director
Conductor: *Jenůfa*
1973, 76 *Capriccio*
1975 *Eugene Onegin*
1977, 79 *Die schweigsame Frau*
1978, 80 *Die Zauberflöte*
1980 *Falstaff*
1985 *Arabella*
1986 *Don Giovanni*
1988 *Kát'a Kabanová*

Sylvain Cambreling
Conductor: *The Rake's Progress*
1981, 82 *Il barbiere di Siviglia*

Jane Glover
Conductor: *A Midsummer Night's
Dream*
1982 *Il barbiere di Siviglia*
1982 *Don Giovanni*
1983 *Die Entführung aus dem Serail*
1984, 86 (Hong Kong) *A
Midsummer Night's Dream*
1985, 86 *Albert Herring*

Graeme Jenkins
Conductor: *Arabella*
Musical Director, Glyndebourne
Touring Opera
1987 *Carmen*
1987 *Capriccio*
1988 *Falstaff*
1988 *L'heure espagnole*
1988 *L'enfant et les sortilèges*

Hermann Michael
Conductor: *Orfeo ed Euridice*
Glyndebourne debut

168

Simon Rattle CBE
Conductor: *Le nozze di Figaro*
1977 *The Cunning Little Vixen*
1980 *La fedeltà premiata*
1981 *Ariadne auf Naxos*
1982 *Der Rosenkavalier*
1983 *L'Amour des Trois Oranges*
1985 *Idomeneo*
1986 *Porgy and Bess*
1987 *L'heure espagnole, L'enfant et les sortilèges*

Sophie Baker

John Cox
Director: *Arabella, The Rake's Progress*
1970 *Il turco in Italia*
1971, 72, 81 *Ariadne auf Naxos*
1972 *Die Entführung aus dem Serail*
1973, 74 *The Visit of the Old Lady*
1973, 76, 87 *Capriccio*
1974 *Idomeneo*
1974, 75, 83 *Intermezzo*
1975, 77, 78, 80 (Paris) *The Rake's Progress*
1977, 79 *Die schweigsame Frau*
1978, 80 *Die Zauberflöte*
1978 *La Bohème*
1979, 80 *La fedeltà premiata*
1980, 82 *Der Rosenkavalier*
1981, 82 *Il barbiere di Siviglia*
1983, 85 *La Cenerentola*
1984, 85 *Arabella*

Donald Southern

Monique Wagemakers
Revival Director &
Choreographer: *Arabella*
First Glyndebourne season: 1983

Jaap Pieper

Christopher Newell
Associate Director: *A Midsummer Night's Dream*
First Glyndebourne season: 1983

Ivor Bolton
Conductor: *Orfeo ed Euridice*
Chorus Master
Glyndebourne Festival debut
First Glyndebourne season: 1982
1985 Jani Strasser Award

Nikolaus Lehnhoff
Director: *Jenůfa*
1988 *Kát'a Kabanová*

Erika Davidson

Michael McCaffery
Director: *Orfeo ed Euridice*
First Glyndebourne season: 1981

Stephen Lawless
Director of Production,
Glyndebourne Touring Opera
Associate Director: *Le nozze di Figaro*
First Glyndebourne season: 1976

Dagmar Thole
Associate Director: *Jenůfa*
First Glyndebourne Season: 1988

Anthony Crickmay

John Bury OBE
Design & Lighting: *Orfeo ed Euridice, A Midsummer Night's Dream*
1970, 71, 74 *La Calisto*
1972, 73, 79 *Il ritorno d'Ulisse in patria*
1973, 74, 76, 81, 84 *Le nozze di Figaro*
1977, 78, 82, 86 *Don Giovanni*
1978, 79, 84, 87 *Così fan tutte*
1979, 81 *Fidelio*
1981, 84, 86 (Hong Kong) *A Midsummer Night's Dream*
1982 *Orfeo ed Euridice*
1984, 86 *L'incoronazione di Poppea*
1985, 87 *Carmen*

John Gunter
Designer: *Le nozze di Figaro*
1985, 86 *Albert Herring*
1986 *Simon Boccanegra*
1986, 87 *Porgy and Bess* (sets)
1987, 88 *La traviata*
1988 *Falstaff*

Jerry Sohn

David Hockney
Designer: *The Rake's Progress*
1975, 77, 78, 80 (Paris) *The Rake's Progress*
1978, 80 *Die Zauberflöte*

Oliver Herrmann

Tobias Hoheisel
Designer: *Jenůfa*
1988 *Kát'a Kabanová*

Donald Southern

Julia Trevelyan Oman CBE
Designer: *Arabella*
1984, 85 *Arabella*

Ben Johnson

Robert Bryan
Lighting Designer: *Arabella, The Rake's Progress*
First Glyndebourne season: 1972

Wolfgang Göbbel
Lighting Designer: *Jenůfa*
First Glyndebourne season: 1988

Deirdre Hall

Paul Pyant
Lighting Designer: *Le nozze di Figaro*
First Glyndebourne season: 1974

Jenny Weston
Choreographer: *Orfeo ed Euridice, A Midsummer Night's Dream, Le nozze di Figaro*
First Glyndebourne season: 1983

Martin Isepp
Head of Music Staff
First Glyndebourne season: 1957

Jonathan Hinden
Chief Coach
First Glyndebourne season: 1966

Jean Mallandaine
Chief Coach
First Glyndebourne season: 1966

Peter Elkus

Craig Rutenberg
Chief Coach
First Glyndebourne season: 1979

Arthur Elgort

David Angus
Chorus Master
First Glyndebourne season: 1989

Donald Adams (English)
Antonio/*Le nozze di Figaro*
1988 Dikoj/*Kát'a*

Roberta Alexander
(American)
Jenůfa/*Jenůfa*
Glyndebourne debut

Curt Appelgren (Swedish)
Bottom/*A Midsummer Night's Dream*
1979, 81 Rocco/*Fidelio*
1981, 84, 86 (Hong Kong)
Bottom/*Dream*
1982 Basilio/*Barbiere*

Mark Baker (American)
Števa/*Jenůfa*
Glyndebourne debut

Lisa Kohler

Kim Begley (English)
Graf Elemer/*Arabella*
1987 Gastone/*Traviata*

Susan Bickley (English)
Hippolyta/*A Midsummer Night's Dream*
Glyndebourne Festival debut

Peter Thompson

Jeffrey Black (Australian)
Demetrius/*A Midsummer Night's Dream*
1986 Sid/*Herring*

Harolyn Blackwell (American)
Zdenka/*Arabella*
1986 Clara/*Porgy*
1987, 88 Princess/*L'enfant*

Gunnel Bohman (Swedish)
Countess/*Le nozze di Figaro*
Glyndebourne debut

Bengt W. Johansson

Mario Bolognesi (Italian)
Don Basilio/*Le nozze di Figaro*
Glyndebourne debut

Roger Bryson (English)
Quince/*A Midsummer Night's Dream*
1979 Nettuno/*Ulisse*
1980 Armed Man/*Zauberflöte*
1981, 84, 86 (Hong Kong) Quince/*Dream*
1981 Bartolo/*Figaro*
1979, 81 Second Prisoner/*Fidelio*
1982, 83 Herald & Cook/*Oranges*
1982 Notary/*Rosenkavalier*
1983 Lawyer/*Intermezzo*
1984 Lictor/*Poppea*

Michael Chance (English)
Oberon/*A Midsummer Night's Dream*
Glyndebourne debut

Lynne Davies (Welsh)
Jano/*Jenůfa*
Glyndebourne Festival debut

Ryland Davies (Welsh)
Lysander/*A Midsummer Night's Dream*
1965 John Christie Award
1965, 66 Sailor/*Dido*
1966 Priest & Armed Man/*Zauberflöte*
1968, 72, 83 Belmonte/*Entführung*
1969, 84 Ferrando/*Così*
1975 Lensky/*Onegin*
1976 Flamand/*Capriccio*
1980 Tamino/*Zauberflöte*
1981, 84, 86 (Hong Kong) Lysander/*Dream*
1982, 83 Prince/*Trois Oranges*
1988 Tichon/*Kát'a*

Robert Cahn

Cynthia Buchan (Scottish)
Hermia/*A Midsummer Night's Dream*
1974 Natura/*Calisto*
1974, 75 Resi/*Intermezzo*
1974 Ill's daughter/*Visit*
1975 Olga/*Onegin*
1976 Cherubino/*Figaro*
1981, 84, 86 (Hong Kong) Hermia/*Dream*
1985 Jennie/*Higglety*
1987 Child/*L'heure*

Deirdre Crowley (Irish)
Aunt/*Jenůfa*
Glyndebourne debut

Menai Davies (Welsh)
Barena/*Jenůfa*
Glyndebourne Festival debut

Ian Laurence

Drahomíra Drobková
(Czechoslovakian)
Grandmother Buryja/*Jenůfa*
Glyndebourne debut

Dale Duesing (American)
Figaro/*Le nozze di Figaro*
1976 Olivier/*Capriccio*
1981, 84, 86 (Hong Kong) Demetrius/*Dream*
1981 Harlekin/*Ariadne*
1984, 86 Ottone/*Poppea*
1987 Guglielmo/*Così*

Gerald Finley (Canadian)
Graf Dominik/*Arabella*
Glyndebourne Festival debut

Elizabeth Gale (English)
Tytania/*A Midsummer Night's Dream*
1974 John Christie Award
1973 Papagena/*Zauberflöte*
1973, 74 Barbarina/*Figaro*
1974 Susanna/*Figaro*
1974, 75, 83 Anna/*Intermezzo*
1976, 77 Nannetta/*Falstaff*
1977, 78, 82 Zerlina/*Don Giovanni*
1979, 81 Marzelline/*Fidelio*
1982 Amor/*Orfeo*
1984, 86 Drusilla/*Poppea*
1984, 86 (Hong Kong)
Tytania/*Dream*
1985, 86 Miss
Wordsworth/*Herring*

Andrew Gallacher (English)
Snug/*A Midsummer Night's Dream*
1981, 84, 86 (Hong Kong)
Snug/*Dream*
1982 Police Inspector/
Rosenkavalier
1983 Opera Singer/*Intermezzo*
1985 Pig-in-Sandwich Board,
Low voice of Ash Tree/*Higglety*

Elisabeth Glauser (Swiss)
Adelaide/*Arabella*
1985 Adelaide/*Arabella*

John Graham-Hall (English)
Flute/*A Midsummer Night's Dream*
Don Curzio/*Le nozze di Figaro*
1985, 86 Albert/*Herring*
1988 Váňa/*Kát'a*

Marion Kistler

Ernst Gutstein (Austrian)
Graf Waldner/*Arabella*
1985 Graf Waldner/*Arabella*
1987 La Roche/*Capriccio*

Alison Hagley (English)
Karolka/*Jenůfa*
Barbarina/*Le nozze di Figaro*
Glyndebourne Festival debut

Clive Barda

John Hancorn (English)
Starveling/*A Midsummer Night's Dream*
Glyndebourne Festival debut

Sophie Baker

Enid Hartle (English)
Fortune-teller/*Arabella*
1970 Natura/*Calisto*
1971 Governess/*Queen of Spades*
1971, 72 Dryade/*Ariadne*
1971 Eternità/*Calisto*
1973 Third Lady/*Zauberflöte*
1975, 77 Forester's Wife, Owl,
Woodpecker/*Vixen*
1977, 79 Carlotta/*Schweigsame Frau*
1984, 85 Fortune-teller/*Arabella*
1987, 88 Annina/*Traviata*

Cynthia Haymon (American)
Euridice/*Orfeo ed Euridice*
1986, 87 Bess/*Porgy*

Robert Hayward (English)
Theseus/*A Midsummer Night's Dream*
Glyndebourne Festival debut

Anne Howells (English)
Baba the Turk/*The Rake's Progress*
1966 Second Boy/*Zauberflöte*
1967, 68 Erisbe/*L'Ormindo*
1969 Dorabella/*Così*
1970, 71 Cathleen/*Rising*
1971 Composer/*Ariadne*
1972, 73 Minerva/*Ulisse*
1974 Diana/*Calisto*
1987 Clairon/*Capriccio*
1988 Meg/*Falstaff*

David Kuebler (American)
Matteo/*Arabella*
1976 Ferrando/*Così*
1987 Flamand/*Capriccio*

Philip Langridge (English)
Laca/*Jenůfa*
1977, 78 Don Ottavio/*Don Giovanni*
1983, 85 Idomeneo/*Idomeneo*

Sunny Joy Langton
(American)
Fiakermilli/*Arabella*
Glyndeboune Festival debut

Sergei Leiferkus (Russian)
Mandryka/*Arabella*
Glyndebourne debut

Felicity Lott (English)
Arabella/*Arabella*
1977, 78, 80 (Paris) Anne/*Rake*
1978 Pamina/*Zauberflöte*
1980, 82 Oktavian/*Rosenkavalier*
1981 Countess/*Figaro*
1981 Helena/*Dream*
1983 Christine/*Intermezzo*
1985 Arabella/*Arabella*
1986 Elvira/*Don Giovanni*
1987 Countess/*Capriccio*

Alastair Miles (English)
Graf Lamoral/*Arabella*
Madhouse keeper/*The Rake's Progress*
Glyndebourne Festival debut

François Loup (French)
Dr Bartolo/*Le nozze di Figaro*
1987, 88 Don Inigo/*L'heure*
1987, 88 Armchair, Tree/*L'enfant*

Sylvia McNair (American)
Anne Trulove/*The Rake's Progress*
Glyndebourne debut

Christian Steiner

Diana Montague (English)
Orfeo/*Orfeo ed Euridice*
1979 L'Humana fragiltà/*Ulisse*

Alexander Oliver (Scottish)
Sellem/*The Rake's Progress*
1970, 73 Monostatos/*Zauberflöte*
1970, 71 Brother Timothy/*Rising*
1971, 72, 81 Dancing
Master/*Ariadne*
1972, 73, 79 Irò/*Ulisse*
1974 Arbace/*Idomeneo*
1974, 75 Baron
Lummer/*Intermezzo*
1981 Scaramuccio/*Ariadne*
1985 Mr Upfold/*Herring*

Clive Barda

Linda Ormiston (Scottish)
Mayor's Wife/*Jenůfa*,
Mother Goose/*The Rake's Progress*
1988 Fekluša/*Kát'a*

Felicity Palmer (English)
Marcellina/*Le nozze di Figaro*
1985 Florence Pike/*Herring*
1988 Kabanicha/*Kát'a*
1988 Mistress Quickly/*Falstaff*

Cornel Lucas

Robert Poulton (English)
Foreman/*Jenůfa*
1987 Esso/Glyndebourne
Touring Opera Singers' Award
1988 John Christie Award
1988 Kuligin/*Kát'a*

Fritz Curzon

Sarah Pring (English)
Maid/*Jenůfa*
1988 Little Owl/*L'enfant*

Deborah Rees (Welsh)
Amor/*Orfeo ed Euridice*
1980 Esso-Glyndebourne Award
1980 First Boy/*Zauberflöte*
1981 Najade/*Ariadne*
1981 Barbarina/*Figaro*
1982 Sophie/*Rosenkavalier*
1985 The Potted Plant, Baby,
Mother Goose/*Higglety*

David Rendall (English)
Tom Rakewell/*The Rake's
Progress*
1976 Ferrando/*Così*
1988 Belmonte/*Entführung*

Joan Rodgers (English)
Susanna/*Le nozze di Figaro*
Glyndebourne debut

Marianne Rorholm (Danish)
Cherubino/*Le nozze di Figaro*
Glyndebourne debut

Tom Gläser

Peter Rose (English)
Trulove/*The Rake's Progress*
1986 (Hong Kong)
Commendatore/*Don Giovanni*

Gordon Sandison (Scottish)
Mayor/*Jenůfa*
1982 Masetto/*Don Giovanni*
1985, 87 Dancaïre/*Carmen*
1987 Douphol/*Traviata*

William Shimell (English)
Count Almaviva/*Le nozze di Figaro*
1984 Count Almaviva/*Figaro*
1986 (Hong Kong) Don Giovanni/*Don Giovanni*

Anja Silja (German)
Kostelnička/*Jenůfa*
Glyndebourne debut

Annegeer Stumphius (Dutch)
Helena/*A Midsummer Night's Dream*
Glyndebourne Festival debut

Anne Kirchbach

Adrian Thompson (English)
Snout/*A Midsummer Night's Dream*
1981, 84, 86 (Hong Kong) Snout/*Dream*
1986 Mr Upfold/*Herring*

Nigel Luckhurst

Jeffrey Wells (American)
Nick Shadow/*The Rake's Progress*
Glyndebourne debut

Miss Janet Moores was awarded the MBE in the New Year Honours List for her services to Glyndebourne since 1934.

We record with sorrow the deaths in the past year of Mrs Almond, Jean-Pierre Ponnelle and Dr T J Walsh.

Gerry Almond's Merton House in Ringmer was a home-from-home to generations of singers from all over the world; for many of them, paying their first visit to this country, her warm friendliness and hospitality provided the perfect support for their British stage debut. A number of singers continued to return to her over the many years of their Glyndebourne engagements.

The distinguished international director and designer Jean-Pierre Ponnelle directed only one production here: an unforgettable *Falstaff* first given in 1976 and twice revived.

Tom Walsh confounded the operatic world by founding the Wexford Festival in 1951, in many ways modelling it on Glyndebourne, though he concentrated on a repertory of little-known works and the Italian *bel-canto* operas of the mid-19th century.

AT HOME
AND ABROAD

by Anthony Whitworth-Jones

Glyndebourne Touring Opera's twentieth Anniversary season in 1988 was one of its most successful. A number of box office records were broken, and ticket sales as a proportion of total income reached a new level, the highest by a considerable margin achieved by any subsidised touring opera company.

Two foreign visits have been made by GTO since last year's Festival. We took *The Electrification of the Soviet Union* to Berlin in September for two performances in the festival specially presented to celebrate that city's status as Cultural Capital of Europe in 1988. A prize was awarded to us by a jury headed by Götz Friedrich. And in February we took *Albert Herring* to Italy for performances in Rome and in the beautiful jewel of a theatre in Reggio Emilia. A resounding success according to the Italian public, the Italian press, and various restaurant owners who fed us magnificently, particularly in the gastronomic paradise of Emilia Romagna. Invitations have already been received to return to Italy, and also to visit Madrid and Valencia with Tippett's opera *New Year* commissioned by Glyndebourne,

Houston Grand Opera, and the BBC. Another invitation – an extraordinary and immensely exciting one – is for GTO to take *Kát'a Kabanová* to the Kirov Theatre in Leningrad with Sian Edwards who spent two years studying conducting at the Conservatory there. All these projected visits abroad have a feeling of celebration about them, a particular purpose and strong focus. We very much hope they will all materialise.

This year's repertory for GTO includes the two Beaumarchais-inspired operas by Mozart and Rossini in the year of the bi-centenary celebrations of the French Revolution, and a new production of Britten's last opera *Death in Venice*. The idea of our doing *Death in Venice* was conceived for, and will be conducted and directed by, GTO's musical and production directors Graeme Jenkins and Stephen Lawless. It was also conceived as another collaboration with the BBC who will make a television recording of the opera in early January 1990. Robert Tear will sing the role of Aschenbach for the first time.

Grande successo per l'Opera di Glyndebourne alla Filarmonica di Roma con Albert Herring

Albert Herring *curtain call, Rome*

Il gruppo affiatatissimo dei cantanti-attori e la London Sinfonietta han reso irresistibili i tre atti dell'opera

Teatro Valli, Reggio Emilia

Photographs by Guy Gravett

Quella notte brava di Albert il timido

178

GLYNDEBOURNE
Touring Opera

B Britten

DEATH IN VENICE
(new production)

W A Mozart

LE NOZZE DI FIGARO

G Rossini

IL BARBIERE DI SIVIGLIA

The Glyndebourne Touring Opera Orchestra
The London Sinfonietta
The Glyndebourne Chorus

Sussex Season	Glyndebourne	10–16 October
		23–28 October

sponsored by TSB Group

with additional contributions from South East Arts and East Sussex County Council

Kent and Sussex Schools Festival	Glyndebourne	17–21 October
Plymouth	Theatre Royal	31 October–4 November
Oxford	Apollo Theatre	7–11 November
Southampton	Mayflower Theatre	14–18 November
Manchester	Palace Theatre	21–25 November
Norwich	Theatre Royal	28 November–2 December

A leaflet giving details of the Tour is available from the Information Office at Glyndebourne

To join GTO's free Mailing List, write to GTO Mailing List, FREEPOST BR (235), Lewes, East Sussex BN8 4BR

Tickets for the Schools Festival are not available to the general public. Enquiries should be addressed to the County Education Officers of Kent CC in Maidstone or East Sussex CC in Lewes

A lot of excitement and keen anticipation has been generated by the engagement of Sir Peter Maxwell Davies as conductor of *Le nozze di Figaro*. One of the most distinguished composers of our day, he has recently devoted a lot of his time to conducting the classical repertory in concert programmes which include his own concertos for the principals of the Scottish Chamber Orchestra. We look forward enormously to the new insights which he will, I am sure, bring to one of the most popular and regularly performed of all operas.

This year marks the tenth anniversary of the biennial Kent and Sussex Schools Festival: since its foundation in 1979 we have presented 10 different operas embracing repertoire from the classical to the contemporary, to a total audience of nearly 30,000 children. Five performances will be given at Glyndebourne in October for school children, three of *Le*

nozze di Figaro, and two of *Il barbiere di Siviglia*. There has always been a warmly responsive atmosphere at these performances, partly, no doubt, because the children have been so well prepared – better than many an adult opera goer. It is to be regretted that the Education Authorities of Kent and East Sussex decided that they did not wish us to present a performance of *Death in Venice*, one of Britten's finest achievements, based on a classic of European literature, and popularised by, amongst others, Mahler, Visconti and Dirk Bogarde. Their decision has resulted in a transfer of one performance of *Death in Venice* from the Schools Festival to the Sussex Season of performances at the beginning of the tour. Instead of three performances for the general public and one for the school children, there will now be four for the public, and we shall make special efforts through our Education Department to encourage older children to attend.

Set model by Tobias Hoheisel for Death in Venice

I would like, here, to express GTO's gratitude to all those Members of the Festival Society who contributed so generously to the Arts Council's Incentive Funding Scheme. Some £50,000 has been raised, to be used over a four year period starting this year. We are always trying to raise the standards of GTO within the welcome constraints of its founding policy to promote young artists. More rehearsal time is now given, particularly for orchestral rehearsal, and almost all improvements we strive to achieve have financial implications. The extent of the contributions from Festival Society Members indicates a clear understanding of the important role played by GTO, not just for its own sake – although that would be enough – but for the artistic health of the Festival. GTO would not exist without the Festival, and the Festival would be significantly the poorer without GTO. The two are interdependent artistically, socially and economically.

I M Abram Esq
John Amphlet Esq
Lord Avebury
John A D Bankes Esq
Mr & Mrs Nicholas Baring
Dr E D Barlow
E G Beaumont Esq
Dr E W Bedford-Turner
A P J Benard Esq
Sir Isaiah Berlin
Mrs R K T Berry
H R D Billson Esq
Adrian Bird Esq
Dr R D Blachford
Gordon S Blacker Esq
Mrs Joan G Blacker
J M Bowers Esq
S J Box Esq
K A Boyes Esq
P M Brown Esq
A L Burn Esq
Lord Carr of Hadley
Dr C H Catlin
Mrs Mary Fiske Cecil
Mrs Margaret Charlton
Richard Charnley Esq
K R Chaundy Esq
A F Bessemer Clark Esq
Colin Clark Esq
G T Clark Esq
Mrs P E Clayton
The Sidney & Elizabeth Corob Charitable Trust
Mrs Marjorie E Crittal
J O Robertson Darby Esq
Dr A M Dawson
Miss E D B Dearn
Mrs R Dell
Dr L A G Dresel
Raymond H Eaton-Williams Esq
H E Evans Esq
D R Fendick Esq
Joseph Fitton Esq

R A Fleming-Williams Esq
W F P Gammie Esq
Dr A Ward Gardner
Dr H C Giordani
John R Goodyear Esq
Miss Irene Gordon
John Gorman Esq QC
Mrs Muriel Grunfeld
Dr David Harper
Sir Frank Hartley CBE
Mrs Joan M Henderson
C G Heselton Esq
Dr S J Hobson
Sir John Hogg
J L Homfray Esq
A S Hooper Esq
A H Isaacs Esq
Sir Clifford Chetwood
Mrs Rosemary Jameson
Mrs Annely Juda
Mrs V L Knox
P L O Leaver Esq
Arnold Lee Esq
Miss P Lee
Morris Leigh Esq PhD
The Rt Hon Robin Leigh-Pemberton
Sidney Leon Esq
Peter T Lewis Esq
Mrs M Lyell
N F McCarthy Esq
F C McDowell Esq
Dr D S J Maw
P E Middleton Esq
S J Mosley Esq
I D F Moss Esq
Dr I S Moss
Lady J Mount
C K Murray Esq
G M Nissen Esq
Mrs John Oldacre
Dr Julia Trevelyan Oman CBE
Sir David Orr
D T Peers Esq

A J Pennell Esq
N H Porter Esq
Dr M W Potts
Mrs J M Powell
The Rt Hon Lord Justice Purchas
W M Pybus Esq
S Douglas Rae Esq
D J Rendell Esq
Mrs E K Roberts
Mrs C Rosefield
Stephen Rosefield Esq
Simon Rothery Esq
J G Rudman Esq
J R Salter Esq
M L H Sankey Esq
Miss Barbara Scott
D J B Seaton Esq
G E Segrove Esq
Mrs F V F Shaw
John C Shaw Esq
Miss Joanna Smith
Sterling Homes Limited
D R R Sutcliffe Esq
Cyril Sweett Esq
Mrs E E Tankard
His Honour Judge Ivor Taylor
Anthony Thornton Esq
Howard J Townson Esq
E W Trafford Esq
Sir Ian Trethowan
C Tytherleigh Esq
R P Vickers Esq
Robert Lewis Vigars Esq
Mrs K B Walsh
M W Warburg Esq
Dr G T Whitaker
Humphrey Whitbread Esq
Mrs J M Wilkes
Mrs June M Williams
R A K Wright Esq
J R Young Esq
G J Zunz Esq

Glyndebourne

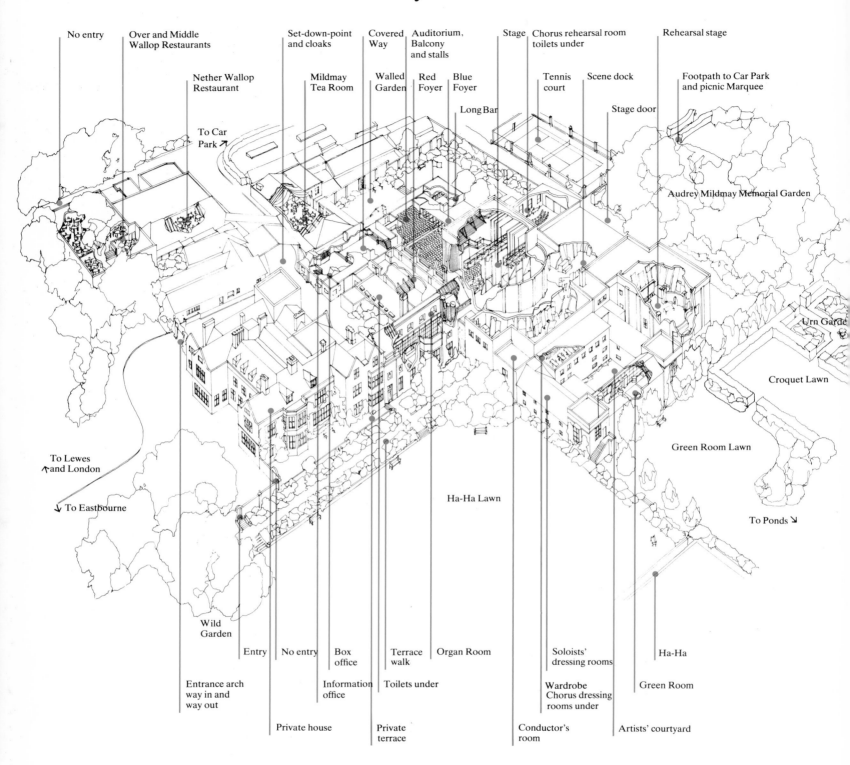

No entry

Over and Middle
Wallop Restaurants

Nether Wallop
Restaurant

To Car
Park ↗

Set-down-point
and cloaks

Mildmay
Tea Room

Covered
Way

Walled
Garden

Auditorium,
Balcony
and stalls

Red
Foyer

Blue
Foyer

Long Bar

Stage

Chorus rehearsal room
toilets under

Tennis
court

Scene dock

Stage door

Rehearsal stage

Footpath to Car Park
and picnic Marquee

Audrey Mildmay Memorial Garden

Urn Garde

Croquet Lawn

Green Room Lawn

To Ponds ↘

Ha-Ha Lawn

To Lewes
↑ and London

↓ To Eastbourne

Wild
Garden

Entry

No entry

Box
office

Information
office

Terrace
walk

Toilets under

Organ Room

Soloists'
dressing rooms

Wardrobe
Chorus dressing
rooms under

Ha-Ha

Green Room

Entrance arch
way in and
way out

Private house

Private
terrace

Conductor's
room

Artists' courtyard

The fold-out illustration opposite
is a quarter-size reproduction of a drawing
by Paul Draper commissioned for Glyndebourne
by Reuters. A limited edition of 200 signed prints
(885 × 630mm) of the ink and water colour
original is on sale through the Glyndebourne
Information Office.

© Reuters Ltd 1983 Designed by Pentagram

How to get there

By road

Glyndebourne is 54 miles from London, 11 miles from Brighton, 14 miles from Eastbourne and 4 miles from Lewes.

Patrons coming by car from London should allow at least 2½ hours driving time from crossing the Thames to Glyndebourne. Traffic is always heavier on Fridays, so please allow additional time.

There are permanent signposts on all main roads leading to Glyndebourne within a radius of 2 miles, and Glyndebourne is marked on most road maps.

From Central and West London the simplest route is by the A23/M23/A23 to Brighton. After entering the Brighton boundary, continue straight across the first set of traffic lights and take the next major turning left at the mini roundabout (Carden Avenue). Follow signs for Lewes, stay on the A27 Lewes Bypass, then turn left onto the A26 Tunbridge Wells road. Turn right after the tunnel and fork right at the top of the hill onto the B2192, then follow signposts to Glyndebourne.

From Eastern London and East Anglia, take the Dartford Tunnel/M25 to junction 6, then A22 to East Grinstead and Uckfield, A26 towards Lewes, turn left to Ringmer (signposted Glyndebourne).

If coming through Lewes Town Centre, follow the signposts for Tunbridge Wells (A26) through the one way system. Just after leaving the town boundary, fork right onto the B2192 and follow the signposts to Glyndebourne.

Car parking facilities are available at a charge of £1; car parking is free to members with Festival Society badges.

Helicopters may land by prior permission only. For further information, details of landing fees and insurance requirements, please contact the Glyndebourne Transport Office (0273 812321).

By train

There are train services from London (Victoria) to Lewes with motor coach connections to and from Glyndebourne. The journey from Victoria to Glyndebourne normally takes about 80 minutes. All recommended down trains call at East Croydon, Gatwick Airport and Haywards Heath. Up trains stop in addition at Clapham Junction. Combined Rail-Coach tickets may be obtained at the Booking Offices of Victoria and East Croydon Stations; coach tickets only may be obtained on the coach. Only recommended trains are met by coaches at Lewes Station.

Patrons are warned that performances cannot be delayed if trains are late, nor can return trains be guaranteed by Glyndebourne. There are usually alternative trains via Brighton if cancellations occur, resulting in later arrival.

Passengers are strongly advised to check with British Rail in advance, particularly if travelling at weekends, as on some Saturdays and Sundays trains may be delayed or diverted due to engineering work on the line.
(British Rail 01–928 5100).

When you are there

Evening dress (black tie/long or short dress) is customary but not obligatory.

The taking of photographs and the use of recording equipment in the auditorium are forbidden.

Latecomers are not permitted into the auditorium after the performance has begun. They will be shown to the Organ Room to which the performance is relayed by television. When a suitable pause occurs the Ushers will direct them to their seats in the auditorium; for many operas this is not before the Long Interval. Members of the audience are advised to arrive at Glyndebourne at least 15 minutes before the time of Curtain Up. Those who wish to leave the auditorium during a performance cannot be re-admitted unless there is a suitable pause.

The Organ Room is open only to opera ticket holders.

Bells, clearly audible in all parts of the gardens (but not necessarily in a closed car in the Car Park) are rung ten, five and three minutes before the rise of the curtain at the beginning of the opera and at the end of all intervals – but not after short pauses in the performance.

Picnics (which are not available for purchase on the premises) may be taken in the gardens, in the John Player Marquee Pavilion adjoining the Car Park, or in Mildmay Hall. Picnic accommodation cannot be reserved in advance, and patrons picnicking are expected to take any litter away with them, litter receptacles not being provided. It is emphasised that it is a private garden and all users are expected to respect it as such.

The restaurants will be open for Dinner during the Long Interval. Tea will be available in Mildmay Hall before all performances. Full details of dining facilities and the ordering of dinners and wines is sent to all ticket holders who are recommended to make their reservations as early as possible.

Telephone enquiries and reservations Ringmer (0273) 812510.

The Long Bar is open before the performance, during the intervals and after the performance, during permitted hours.

Members of the audience are requested to refrain from wearing watches which have automatic time signals as these are known to disturb other patrons.

The Management cannot accept responsibility for loss or damage to articles left in the gardens or on the premises. Enquiries about Lost Property should be made to the Information Office, which is open from 10am to 5pm (until curtain down on days of performance).

Facilities for the disabled. Both sides of the Stalls are accessible to wheelchairs (limited to two on each side), and there is a special lavatory for the disabled near the Transport Office. Please ask Ushers for assistance if required.

Refreshments are available for chauffeurs in Mildmay Hall during the first half of the performance.

Dogs must not be brought into the grounds, gardens or Car Park.

On sale through the Information Office

The Information Office and Shop is open from 10am (12.30 on Sundays) to the end of the performance: non-performance days 10am to 5pm.

Orders by post should be addressed to the Information Office, Glyndebourne, Lewes, East Sussex BN8 5UU. Remittances should be made payable to 'Glyndebourne'.

For a full list of merchandise available by post, please send sae to the Information Office.

Records

Porgy and Bess

The EMI recording with the 1986 Glyndebourne cast conducted by Simon Rattle was made in London in January 1987 and will be released this summer
LP   £18.99 by post £21.50
Cassette £18.99 by post £20
CD   £32.50 by post £33.50

Glyndebourne Plate

Glyndebourne has commissioned Spode to produce a limited edition of 500 8" bone china plates with a drawing by Sir Hugh Casson and 22 carat gold border £27.50
By recorded delivery post £29.75

Programme Books

1989 edition: £6 by post £8.50
Back numbers of most issues are available at prices according to their relative scarcity value.
Binders for Glyndebourne Festival Programme Books, each holding 8 to 10 copies £4 by post £5.25

Mozart design cards

Greetings cards with costume designs from Mozart productions at Glyndebourne: Osmin *Die Entführung aus dem Serail* (designs by Oliver Messel, Emanuele Luzzati and William Dudley) Figaro and Susanna *Le nozze di Figaro* (designs by Oliver Messel, Elizabeth Bury and John Gunter)
£1.95 per pack of three by post £2.25

Libretti

ENO/Royal Opera Guides to *Jenůfa*, *Le nozze di Figaro* and *Arabella*, and English texts of *Orfeo ed Euridice*, *A Midsummer Night's Dream* and *The Rake's Progress*

Gallery

Manager: Rosy Runciman

Red Foyer
This year there is an exhibition of costume designs by Elizabeth Bury, John Gunter and Tobias Hoheisel in the red foyer together with a selection of Sir Hugh Casson's vignettes of life in this country and abroad. The Witch Ball Antique Print Gallery has a varied exhibition of theatrical prints, all of which are for sale.

Blue Foyer
The blue foyer takes on a fresh look. We have invited a number of artists, some of whom will be familiar to Glyndebourne patrons and some totally new, to paint those scenes of Glyndebourne which particularly appeal to them. The result is, we hope, a lively exhibition having direct relevance to everyone visiting Glyndebourne.

In addition, in both foyers, there are small displays of hand engraved glass depicting the house, coat of arms and operatic characters.

Video recordings

The following Glyndebourne productions are currently available on video cassette in VHS format only:

Pickwick Video
@ £12.99 by post £14.50

Macbeth
Le nozze di Figaro
Il ritorno d'Ulisse in patria
Idomeneo (1974)
Così fan tutte
Falstaff
Don Giovanni
Die Zauberflöte
Fidelio
Die Entführung aus dem Serail
La traviata

NVC/Castle Communications
@ £14.99 by post £16.50

Il barbiere di Siviglia
A Midsummer Night's Dream
Orfeo ed Euridice
L'Amour des Trois Oranges
Idomeneo (1983)
La Cenerentola
Intermezzo
Arabella
L'incoronazione di Poppea
Where the Wild Things Are/Higglety Pigglety Pop!
Albert Herring
Carmen

Lectures

Else Mayer-Lismann MBE, Artistic Director of the Mayer-Lismann Workshop, will give explanatory lectures with musical examples on the operas to be performed during the Glyndebourne Festival. Tickets and further information from Ruth Wing, Hon Secretary 21 Sussex Mansions, Old Brompton Road London SW7 3LB